FRENCH COOKBOOK

Made Simple, at Home

The Complete Guide Around France to the Discovery of the Tastiest Traditional Recipes Such as Homemade Cassoulet, Crepes, Ratatouille and Much More

Chef MARINO

bng-books.com

Acknowledgment

I want to thank you for buying my book and for trusting in me, sincerely ...Thanks!

Writing a book is harder than I thought and more rewarding than I could have ever imagined.
My thanks go to all of you, readers, I thank you because without you I could not be what I am, without you my books simply…would not exist!
I would like to introduce you all my works, and, if you like them, invite you to leave a positive thought; this will help me to continue my work and will help other people to buy what they are looking for!

Again…Thanks You!

Chef Marino

Click to see all my books
bng-books.com

French Cookbook

Chef Marino

TABLE OF CONTENTS

ORIGINS OF FRENCH CUISINE 7

REGIONAL FRENCH CUISINE...13

CHARACTERISTICS OF FRENCH CUISINE 20

MEALS 25

    COQUILLES SAINT-JACQUES 25
    BAKED CAMEMBERT..27
    MOULESÀLAMARINIÈRES 29
    BAKED POMMES FRITES 31
    BUCKWHEAT CRÊPES 32
    BLANQUETTE DE VEAU...33
    SOLE MEUNIÈRE 36
    HACHISPARMENTIER 37
    BOUDIN NOIR AUX POMMES 39
    CHEESE SOUFFLÉ 41
    STEAK TARTARE 43
    POT-AU-FEU 44
    BASQUE PIPERADE..48
    MAGRET DE CANARD 50
    GARBURE 52
    CASSOULET...54
    PAN-SEARED FOIE GRAS..56
    CONFIT DE CANARD 58
    POULETBASQUAISE 61
    LAMPREY À LA BORDELAISE 62
    QUENELLES OF PIKE WITH LOBSTER SAUCE..64
    GIGOT D'AGNEAUPLEUREUR..67
    BOUILLABAISSE 69
    PISSALADIÈRE 72
    RATATOUILLE 74
    ROASTED CHICKEN AND GARLIC 75
    NAVARIND'AGNEAU (NAVARIN OFLAMB)...76
    FOIE DE VEAU À LA LYONNAISE 78

French Cookbook

ALIGOT 80

FONDUE SAVOYARDE 81

TARTIFLETTE 82

GRATIN DAUPHINOIS (POTATO GRATIN).. 84

COQ AU VIN 86

OIGNONSGLACÉS A BRUN [BROWN-BRAISED ONIONS] 89

CHAMPIGNONS SAUTÉS AU BUERRE [SAUTÉED MUSHROOMS] 90

FLAMMEKUECHE.. 91

RACLETTE 93

CHOUCROUTE GARNIE 95

BAECKEOFFE.. 97

QUICHE LORRAINE 99

SOUP 101

SOUPE À L'OIGNON 101

SOUPE DE POISSON 103

ROUILLE 105

SOUPE AU PISTOU... 107

DESSERTS... 109

BÛCHE DE NOËL 109

TARTETATIN 113

CHERRY CLAFOUTIS 115

ROASTED RHUBARB CLAFOUTI 115

CRÊPES SUZETTE... 118

PARIS-BREST 120

MINI GÂTEAU PARIS-BREST 122

CHOCOLATE ÉCLAIRS 124

KOUIGNAMANN 127

CREMEBRULEE 130

PITHIVIERS 132

FRENCH APPLE CAKE 134

FAR-BRETON 136

GATEAU BASQUE.. 138

YOGURT CAKE.. 141

FRENCH APPLE TART 143

TARTE AU CITRON 145

FRENCH STRAWBERRY PIE 146

BASQUE PUMPKIN CORNBREAD 148

CANELÉS 150

BUGNES 152

NAVETTES DE MARSEILLE 154

PROFITEROLES 155

A BEAUMES DE VENISE CAKE 157

A TARTETROPÉZIENNE 159

MACARON 162

FRENCH ALMOND NOUGAT 164

RELIGIEUSE 166

FIG TART 169

GATEAU SAINT-HONORE 171

MADELEINES 177

SAVOY CAKE 179

FROMAGE BLANC 181

CHOCOLATE MOUSSE 183

KOUGLOF ALSATIAN BRIOCHE 185

MONT BLANC 187

MÄNNELE (ST. NICHOLAS BREAD) 190

DAMSON PIE 192

TARTE FRANGIPANE MIRABELLES 193

Origins of FRENCH Cuisine

The concept of haute cuisine has always been associated with France and, if you notice, words like chef and nouvelle cousine, even if you do it on purpose, are French. Many of the most famous chefs in the world are also French and some sauces and preparations that are famous all-over the world come from France. But where does this way of cooking come from and where does its most ancient traditions sink?

This is because French cuisine has a very long history and an eno-gastronomic tradition that ranges from the cheeses that have made it famous all-over the world to the numerous wines appreciated by many. Yet, the first great basic contradiction, French cuisine does not exist. Or rather, there is not a single French cuisine, but many variations that reflect the diversity of the French regions and their most characteristic dishes.

We are therefore talking about typical local dishes that, all together, have contributed to making the French cuisine famous all-over the world and a symbol of different dishes that are born in different places with different climates and cultures. They all have a long history behind them in which flavor and refinement have their roots in the monarchy and in the French Revolution, although there is no lack of influence given by the colonies and proximity to other cultures, including the Italian one.

The first news of French cuisine is in the Middle Ages and Caterina de' Medici had great influence in this regard, who brought the tradition of Tuscan cuisine as a dowry to Henry II of France. The sovereign was a great lover of cooking, so much so that she opened a school that bore her name and made substantial changes in the way of conceiving the table, such as the order of the dishes to be served and the choice of combining certain foods.

Banquets were very popular among the aristocracy and consisted of several courses that were served to guests at the same time. Meat was one of the main foods, often seasoned with sauces and condiments, along with shortcrust pastry and cheeses, often served with honey.

Versailles, as history teaches us, was a great pole of attraction not only for luxury and splendor known throughout Europe, but also for great attention to the kitchen and the laid tables. The French Revolution is considered a sort of watershed, but it was a historically very important period for French cuisine because in this period the first restaurants were born, in the modern sense in which we know them; the cooks who worked at court, after all, somehow had to invent new ones or, in many other cases, they were the aristocrats fleeing the guillotine and emigrating abroad with their own culinary experience. From the time of the French Revolution there was no longer a single hub, Versailles, but each province and area of France began to outline its own gastronomic characteristics and to develop its own cultures and traditions, the same that have been handed down to us today and that have French cuisine made great in the world.

During the twentieth century, particularly during the 1970s, a movement linked to cooking was born in France and destined to make people talk about it a lot: the Nouvelle Cousine. This type of innovative cuisine was signed by chefs Gault and Millau and immediately represented an innovation in the world, not only in French but also in international cuisine. The canons were completely upset by new presentations, by new dishes and by the resizing of the courses and their size. But not only this; it was also about new recipes, new cooking methods and new tools.

In short, everything was changing in the world of cooking. The ten commandments of the Novelle Cousine were also drawn up, which still represent the foundation of haute cuisine all-over the world and among the great starred chefs:

- Foods should not be cooked for too long.
- Only fresh and high quality products are used.
- The proposed menu must be light.
- You don't have to be systematically modern.
- We must always go in search of new techniques.

- No marinades or aging.
- No sauces or too rich gravies.
- The dietary aspect must always be considered.
- You must not make up the presentation of the dish.
- Yes to inventiveness and creativity.

Even today the Nouvelle Cousine plays a very important role not only for French cuisine, but for that of the great chefs who, from all-over the world, are inspired by her for their haute cuisine according to some fundamental principles:

- Products must always be fresh and of high quality.
- Cooking times must be short.
- The sauces must be light.
- The aesthetics of the presentation plays an important role, as does the flavor.

But French cuisine is not just Nouvelle Cousine, luckily especially in economic terms given the high price of haute cuisine offered by starred chefs from all-over the world. Anyone planning a trip to Paris cannot fail to consider the idea of dining in a bistro, the typical restaurant where you can savor traditional French dishes and flavors wrapped in a relaxing and romantic atmosphere.

Soupsare among the main dishes of France. They can be prepared with onions, beef or fish based, depending on the dish and the recipe. Even the coq au vin, literally translated as cockerel in wine is one of the traditional French dishes.

Obviously, a good selection of French wines cannot be missed.

But the bistro is not the only place in France where you can taste the typical dishes of this land. Another must, in fact, are the brasseries, which we could compare to our pubs, simple and familiar places where you can drink a beer strictly accompanied by a meat dish. You can't miss French fries and a good selection of French cheeses, which can be presented as an aperitif or as an accompaniment to the second course.

But let's not forget that French cuisine is above all known for its sauces, which differ from each other according to the flavor, texture and type of food they accompany. In France, every city has its own sauce. That's right, many different preparations created to accompany meats, first and second courses, but also side dishes and vegetables. Depending on the region to which it belongs, the sauce can be salty or be prepared with oil and spices, seasonal vegetables or fish.

French Cheeses

Finally, it is impossible not to mention the cheeses; French cuisine includes at least 500 varieties only if we exclude all homemade dairy preparations. Along with the Italian ones, French cheeses are known and appreciated all-over the world for their flavor and delicacy.

Alsace, Brittany and the Pyrenees, but also Normandy, Provence and Corsica. In short, in every corner of France a different cheese is produced, an ancient tradition practiced since Roman times. The very first cheeses were produced in terracotta containers, which retained the bacteria produced by the curd, and this technique is still practiced today in some areas of France for the production of some varieties of cheese.

In France, cheese is very important and is considered a food that goes very well with wine, with which you can end a meal in the best way. In restaurants, in general, cheese is served together with bread and sometimes with butter, even according to the dish that has been ordered.

Among the most famous cheeses we certainly find Camembert, produced with the milk of Normandy cows, Brie and Rocquefort, the famous cheese with green veins that originate from the molds that form inside, a bit like our Gorgonzola.

Regional French Cuisine

French cuisine is the result of a long historical tradition and the excellence of its products, the artisans who work them and of course the great chefs celebrated all-over the world.

As a true form of art, UNESCO's patrimonial recognition of French cuisine is also extended to the social context and to the taste of conviviality that arises around a lunch and a beautiful table set, and which is typical of French culture. Among the basic components of this gastronomic reality, Unesco indicates attention to dishes, local products, pairing with wines, the way of setting the table, the gestures of tasting. A traditional ritual that is handed down from generation to generation and strengthens family and social relationships.

On the strength of this important recognition, in 2011 he kicked off the French Gastronomy Festival which is usually celebrated on the third weekend of September throughout France.

Alsace and Lorraine

Alsace and Lorraine have signature dishes, proof of a tradition of parties and banquets. These two regions have a very diverse cuisine well known examples are choucroute (single dish with sauerkraut, potatoes, bacon and pork) and "Quiche Lorraine" (quiche made with cheese, bacon and ham). As for the desserts, apple, plum and blueberry pies abound, the Alsatian brioche and the Kougelhopf, an Alsatian cake in the shape of a crown.

Aquitaine

From the Béarn department in the Basque Country, to the Landes, Bordeaux department, Aquitaine is a real feast for the table. Proud of its traditions and of the products of the earth. Taste is the king of the "art de vivre". Foie gras, duck breast, Bordeaux fillet, "garbure" (cabbage soup), Bayonne ham and Gironde caviar are characteristic products of one of the best French cuisines, without forgetting the Bordeauxe wines Bergerac, with high quality DOP wines. Its wonderful liqueurs based on hazelnut, juniper, plum and raspberry to accompany desserts.

Auvergne

Auvergne is famous for its abundant and rich recipes, for their cold cuts and cheeses: Saint Nectaire, Fourme d'Ambert, Bleu d'Auvergne. With the help of some chefs, Auvergne recipes have become more refined dishes, proving that it is possible to add creativity to tradition. Among the best known are the stew (pork, carrots, potatoes, cabbage, onion), coq au vin and tripoux (beef, bacon, onion, wine). And for desserts you have to try Millards (cherry pie), pompes (apple pie), la Fouasse (brioche), Murat croissants (cream dessert), cream cakes, fruit and desserts.

Brittany

If you love the sea, Brittany is your land. Here you can taste the best oysters and seafood, as well as the Cotriade (fish soup) and the French dessert par excellence: the crepes. But not only, also the galettes, salty crepes and the far, the famous Breton dessert.

Burgundy

The reputation of Burgundy, its wines and its cuisine is long and dates back to the Gallo-Roman period. Proof of this are the culinary badges preserved in the Archaeological Museum of Dijon. Among the most famous recipes of Burgundy are snails, beef bourguignonne and roast beef. Burgundy is obviously synonymous with Dijon mustard, strong or flavored to accompany many dishes of its cuisine.

Loire Valley

The Loire Valley offers many typical products: green lentils, crotin de Chavignol (goat cheese) or Mique (vegetable soup with pork). La Tarte Tatin, the mythical upside-down apple pie, found throughout France is named after its creators, sisters Caroline and Stephaine Tatin. While they were preparing the apple pie, it fell and was put back into the mold but in the opposite direction.

Champagne-Ardenne

Among meat lovers, Champagne-Ardenne is famous for its specialties. First of all the Troyes andouillette, a typical specialty of the city, and the Ardennes ham. It is not possible to go through this region without a champagne tasting, a drink that has become world famous. Another jewel of Champagne-Ardenne is nicknamed gray diamond: the truffle. For desserts you absolutely must taste the Reims biscuits.

Corsica
The traditional Corsican menu consists of meat, seafood, and for dessert a brocain (dessert with sheep or goat's milk). Other typical products are chestnut flour, honey, or Cedrat (a citrus fruit) or myrtle liqueur (based on fruit or flowers).

Languedoc-Roussillon
The cuisine of Languedoc-Roussillon is seasoned with olive oil and aromatic herbs (thyme, rosemary, juniper...) which perfume dishes of game and snails accompanied by tasty vegetables such as aubergines, tomatoes, courgettes, peppers. Fish dishes deserve a special mention: oysters and mussels from Bouzigues, bourride sétoise (monkfish dish accompanied by aioli), octopus tielles (bread dough, octopus, tomatoes, onions, spices), and cod from Nîmes (minced cod with olive oil, milk and garlic). For dessert, you can't resist a crème brulée.

Midi-Pyrenees
In Toulouse, the most important dish is certainly the cassoulet (made of beans, leg of lamb, bacon...). Goose and duck are served confit or as foie gras. Regional specialties include the Tolosa albigeoise duck, and asparagus from the Tarn. In the mountains, the Pyrenees and Aveyron offer a

cuisine of character with tripoux de Naucelles (white wine, ham and garlic), Entraygues or alicuit cold cuts. As for cheeses, the Aubrac area produces the inimitable thick crust Laguiole (which is usually incorporated into garlic mashed potatoes to make aligot) and Millau Roquefort. Wine plays an important role in this region, the wines of Cahors and Bergerac, already famous in Roman times, are wines protected by the designation of origin mark and of great quality.

Nord-Pas de Calais and Picardy

In Nord-Pas de Calais you will appreciate the pleasures of a generous table, characterized by a variety of rich and tasty dishes. Flemish cuisine offers many soups such as Le Touquet's chowder. Starters include "Potjevleesch" (veal, pork, rabbit and chicken terrine), "Flamiche aux Maroilles" (leek pie) or "l'andouille" (a type of sausage). Among the main dishes are the rabbit with plums, the "Hochepot" (stew of beef, lamb, bacon and vegetables), the "ficelle Picarde (crêpe with sauce of ham, bechamel and mushrooms), the typical duck, rabbit, eel and pike.

Normandy

Normandy has many gastronomic treasures, cheeses such as Pont l'Eveque or Livarot, Isigny caramel, liqueurs such as Calvados and cider or the apples with which the famous "Trou Normand" (liqueur, apples, mint, salt and ice water) to drink with a meal to aid digestion.

Pays de la Loire

Here you can taste oysters and seafood, the famous rillettes (homemade pate), accompanied by a good wine from the Anjou region, and finally the typical dessert: the Vendée brioche.

Poitou-Charentes

In the gastronomy of Poitou-Charentes the protagonist is the sea and its products. The typical menu could be: a dozen oysters from Marennes-Oléron with rye bread with Echiré butter, snails (cagouilles), a piece of lamb and finally, a little cabichou cheese.

Provence Alps French Riviera

In the markets of Provence they can buy all the products of the territory: olive oil, herbs of Provence, figs, strawberries from Carpentras, melon from Cavaillon, goat cheese, fish. You cannot leave the region without having tasted its specialties: such as bouillabaisse, a fish soup typical of

Marseille; aïoli, a garlic-based mayonnaise; tapenade, a puree of black olives mixed with capers, anchovies and tuna or even the legendary ratatouille... all accompanied by a Côtes de Provence wine. The specialties of Nice are the pissaladière, a savory pie made with onions, anchovies and black olives, the Nicoise salad consisting of tomatoes, artichokes, peppers, hard-boiled eggs, black olives, olive oil; the pistou, a vegetable soup season with basil, garlic, tomato, olive oil.

Rhône-Alpes

The Rhone valley is a key region in French gastronomy. From Bresse chickens to truffle soup, not forgetting fondue, raclette and gratin dauphinois (a mixture of potatoes, eggs and milk), dishes to be enjoyed in a wooden chalet in the mountains or in one of the typical Lyon bouchons. In this region the richness of natural products generates a variety of dishes to which rich vineyards bring their generous support.

Among the Lyon specialties: baked pike croquettes with butter, Lyon sausage, pérougiennes and bugnes biscuits. The desserts are the most famous of the region are the Montélimar nougat prepared with sugar, honey, eggs, vanilla and almonds and the marrons glacés. The best wines of Rhône-Alpes are Beaujolais and the Côtes du Rhône.

Characteristics of French Cuisine

France (and especially the city of Paris), as we know, is known all-over the world for its history, culture and its fabulous monuments, but its typical dishes and wines have always dominated the rest.

Thanks to its renowned chefs and their menus, served in restaurants located on every continent, French specialties and foods continue to increase their fame and the fame of the chefs who prepared them.

Whether we are talking about appetizers, first courses, main courses, single dishes, side dishes, breakfasts, crepes, savory pies (also called quiche) or salads, French cuisine always has typical dishes belonging to its tradition that can make our meal unique and delight our guests.

When one thinks of the traditional food of French gastronomy, the greedy typical French dishes immediately come to mind, such as delicious chocolate cakes, fruit desserts, soups such as onion soup (the main dish of French cuisine) or parmentier or sauces (such as béchamel) and you can't wait to book a one-way ticket to France and dive into a riot of unique flavors with simple preparation and special taste.

An aspect that unites the cuisine of France and that of Italy is the fact that each region has its own culinary tradition, which varies from region to region, based on natural ingredients, such as eggs, butter, potatoes, milk, chicken, cream, bread, pasta, meat or fish, vegetables (such as courgettes and tomatoes) and seasonal fruit such as strawberries or mushrooms.

Each recipe, belonging to modern French cuisine, originates from the careful study of the characteristics of the ingredients, wisely combined to create an extraordinary balance of flavors even if many of the oldest and most famous traditional gastronomic recipes have been prepared in the kitchens almost by accident or by distraction by chefs or assistant cooks who are a bit clumsy.

Names of typical french dishes

Typical French foods have names that alone attract the hungry international tourist by reputation: bouillabaisse marseillaise, moules frites, ratatouille, tarte tatin, quiche lorraine, Provençal soup, snails, creams and soups and confit de canard. These are just some of the many proposals that can be found on a restaurant menu.

<u>Where to eat the typical dishes of french cuisine</u>
Speaking of restaurants, if you want some advice on where to eat when you stay in Paris, it is a must to have your meals, for lunch or dinner, at least once in the typical and famous bistros: the home atmosphere that is created with the soft lights, the classic furnishings and the traditional Parisian dishes make the time spent inside the restaurant unforgettable.

Among the most famous typical first courses that can be ordered, the soups, both with onions and with fish and beef, the coq au vin, that is the cockerel in wine or the boeuf à the bourguignonne, certainly accompanying them with a good red wine such as Bordeaux.

Even the Parisian brasseries are another fundamental stop on a trip to the capital: this type of place offers connoisseurs the opportunity to taste the best French beers accompanied by an excellent entrecôte and the ever-present pommes frites, our common french fries; on the other hand, those who do not like the strong taste of alcohol can sip the typical apple cider, also suitable for children thanks to its low alcohol content.

In addition to the inevitable meats that make up the main dish, the typical French dinner is first of all articulated with the appetizer, usually consisting of cooked vegetables or meat terrines, and immediately after the meat dish with French cheeses, which are not lacking never on the table.

French Cookbook

Sauces

French cuisine, to accompany all types of meat, from pork to beef and most courses, offers a wide range of sauces.

Each city in France has its own characteristic sauces, from Burgundy to Brittany, specially designed to accompany first courses, main courses or side dishes typical of different geographical areas.

Depending on the region of origin, a sauce can be salty or based on oil and spices, based on fish or seasonal vegetables wisely combined to enhance the typical seasonal specialties.

In any case, you can always be sure that sauces of various types are never lacking to make both meat, fish and game ever tastier and tastier as well as offering a touch of refinement and serving as dressings for salads and other typical preparations of the cuisine of France.

Cheeses

There is also a huge selection of French cheeses which are the most popular with tourists and residents. The most popular traditional cheeses are certainly Brie, Camembert and Roquefort, which are more enhanced when paired with white or rosé wines.

Furthermore, a way to create an ideal, fast and tasty combination, which allows us to best savor these cheeses is to bring them to the table accompanied by platters of cold cuts such as ham or salami which, combined with a freshly cut baguette and accompanied by good beer will make the happiness of all diners.

Sweets

As a delicious snack you can also stop and enjoy delicious sweets such as calissons accompanied by tea such as that typical of the south of France, flavored with lavender.

For breakfast, French cuisine is always able to offer interesting ideas such as croissants, delicious rolls of puff pastry and butter to be stuffed with jams or to be enjoyed as they are and accompanied with orange juice and coffee. During the Christmas period, on the other hand, the classic dishes give way to typical French Christmas dishes that differ from the first ones because they are offered special foods: during the meal the classic meat terrines give way to oysters and foie gras, which the French adore and use on special occasions.

At the end of the meal it is customary to serve a cake or exclusive sweets typical of French pastries such as the croquembouche, composed of many puffs assembled in the shape of a pyramid, filled with cream and covered with caramel or petit four, small flour-based and cooked pasta baked ideal to be enjoyed together with an excellent champagne.

But even among desserts, the French tradition leaves its mark with delicious macarons, sweets or traditional cakes such as tarte tatin, saint honore, tarte tropezien or profitteroles, sweets that make design and refinement their strong point.

Meals

Coquilles Saint-Jacques

Ingredients

6 tbsp. unsalted butter

8 oz. button mushrooms, minced 2 tbsp. minced parsley

3 small shallots, minced Kosher salt and freshly ground black pepper, to taste 1tbsp. minced tarragon, plus 6 whole leaves, to garnish 1 bay leaf

¾ cup dry vermouth

2 tbsp. flour

6 large sea scallops

⅔ cup grated Gruyère

½ cup heavy cream

½ tsp. fresh lemon juice

Instructions

Heat mushrooms, 4 tbsp. butter, and ⅔ of the shallots in a 4-qt. saucepan overmedium heat; cook until the mixture forms a loose paste, about 25 minutes. Stir

parsley and minced tarragon into mushroom mixture; season with salt andpepper. Divide mixture among 6 cleaned scallop shells or shallow gratin dishes.

Bring remaining shallots, vermouth, bay leaf, salt, and ¾ cup water to a boil in a

4-qt. saucepan over medium heat. Add scallops; cook until barely tender, about 2minutes. Remove scallops; place each over mushrooms in shells. Continue boiling cooking liquid until reduced to ½ cup, about 10 minutes; strain. Heatbroiler to high. Heat remaining butter in a 2-qt. saucepan over medium heat. Add flour; cook until smooth, about 2 minutes. Add reduced cooking liquid andcream; cook until thickened, about 8 minutes. Add cheese, juice, salt, and pepper; divide the sauce over scallops. Broil until browned on top, about 3minutes; garnish each with a tarragon leaf.

Baked Camembert

Ingredients
- *1 clove garlic*
- *250 g Camembert*
- *olive oil*
- *a few tips fresh rosemary*
- *afew sprigs rosemary*
- *bite-sized pieces bread, stale*
- *1 tiny pinch sea salt*
- *1 small handful mixed nuts*
- *1 small handful dried cranberries*

Method
Preheat the oven to 180°C/350°F/gas 4. Leaving it in the box, score around thetop of a 250g Camembert about ½cm in and cut off the top layer of skin. Finely slice a peeled garlic clove and poke it into the top of the cheese with a few freshrosemary tips. Drizzle with a little olive oil then bake in the hot oven for 15 to 20 minutes, or until gorgeous and oozy in the middle.

Thread bite-sized pieces of stale bread onto stripped woody rosemary sprigs,drizzle them with olive oil and a tiny pinch of sea salt to help them crisp up thenlay them on a tray and pop in the oven to cook with the Camembert.

Finely chop a small handful of dried cranberries and mixed nuts and put them ina little bowl. Once your bread skewers are golden and crisp and your cheese isoozy, put everything out on a board then dunk a bit of toasted bread in the gooeycheese and dip it in the cranberry and nuts – a little mouthful of 1980s heaven.

Moules*àla*Marinières

Ingredients

An 8-to 10-quart enameled kettle with cover, though I've made this in manyother pots successfully 2 cups light, dry white win or 1 cup dry white vermouth 8 parsley sprigs
1/2 cup minced shallots, or green onions, or very finely minced onions ¼ teaspoon thyme
1/2 bay leaf
6 tablespoons butter
1/8 teaspoon pepper
1/2 cup roughly chopped parsley
6 quarts scrubbed, soaked mussels

Method

Bring all but the last two Ingredients to boil in the kettle. Boil for 2 to 3 minutes
to evaporate its alcohol and to reduce its volume slightly.
Add the mussels to the kettle. Cover tightly and boil quickly over high heat.
Frequently grasp the kettle with both hands, your thumbs clamped to the cover,and toss the mussels in the kettle and an up and down slightly jerky motion so
the mussels will change levels and cook evenly. In about 5 minutes, the shells
will swing open and the mussels are done.

With a big skimmer, dip the mussels into wide soup plates. Allow the cookingliquid to settle for a moment so any sand will sink to the bottom. Then ladle the liquid over the mussels, sprinkle with the parsley and serve immediately.

Baked Pommes Frites

Ingredients

1/4 cup extra-virgin olive oil
6 russet potatoes
Salt and freshly ground black pepper

Method

Preheat the oven to 400 degrees F. Peel potatoes (if peeled fries are your thing,skip it if you couldn't care) and cut into half-inch thick slices (lengthwise) cut
again into 1/2-inch thick fries. Place the potatoes into a pot with cold water and 1tablespoon of salt. Bring up to a gentle boil and simmer until a paring knife tip
goes through easily, cooked about 3/4 of the way through. Drain carefully and put potatoes a bowl. Add olive oil, 1 tablespoon salt, ½ teaspoon black pepper. Toss well and lay out in 1 layer on baking sheet. Bake
until light brown.

Buckwheat Crêpes

Ingredients
3 large eggs
1 1/4 cups buckwheat flour
3/4 cup nonfat milk
1/4 cup vegetable oil plus additional for skillet
1/4 teaspoon salt
1 1/4 cups (or more) water

Preparation
Place flour in medium bowl. Whisk in eggs, 1/4 cup oil, milk, 1 ¼ cups water, and salt.
Heat 10-inch-diameter nonstick skillet over medium-high heat; brushpan with oil. Add 1/4 cupful batter to skillet; tilt to coat bottom. Cookcrepe until golden on bottom, adjusting heat to prevent burning, 30 to
45 seconds. Using spatula, turn crepe over; cook 30 seconds. Transferto plate. Repeat with remaining batter, stacking crepes between sheets
of plastic wrap.

Blanquette de Veau

Ingredients

- *1 pint pearl onions, peeled*
- *D'Artagnan veal tenderloin about 2 ½ lbs., trimmed and cut into cubes andthoroughly rinsed before and after trimming (or veal stew meat or veal cheeks)*
- *6 c stock (veal or chicken)*
- *2 T butter*
- *1 celery stalk cut into sticks*
- *Bouquet garni: 1 thyme sprig, 1 bay leaf,parsley stems, 6 peppercorns, 2 cloves garlic, sliced and 3 cloves tied in cheesecloth or loose*
- *1 small leek, sliced in half in 4" pieces*
- *1 largecarrots, peeled & cut into thick sticks*
- *4 Tablespoons butter*
- *1 teaspoon coarse salt*
- *2 T vermouth*
- *5 Tablespoons flour*
- *1 container veal demi-glace from D'Artagnan the (or 1 cup of your own)*
- *2T Cognac*
- *½ c heavy cream*
- *3 egg yolks*
- *1 Tablespoon lemon juice*
- *2 c sliced mushrooms*
- *minced fresh parsley*
- *salt and pepper to taste*
- *chopped yellow celery tops (optional)*

Preparation

Take the veal cuttings, vegetables, bouquet garni and stock and put in a large pot(a wide-mouthed enamel cast iron pan is perfect). Heat it and simmer onmedium-low for 1½ hours, skimming and checking as you go.

While you are doing this, take ½ c of the stock from the pan and 2 T butter andsimmer the onions covered for 10 minutes. When they are nearly done remove the cover and reduce the liquid till it is syrupy. Remove and reserve the onionsand the glaze.

After 1 ½ hours, strain the stock, pressing on the solids and then discard thevegetables and meat bits. Add the demi-glace to the stock. You should have around 4 cups. You can do all of this the day before so that the dish comestogether quickly before the meal.

Rinse the veal cubes again and add to the stock*. Cook for about 15 minutesover very low heat… barely a simmer. Check it — you want it medium rare (you will need to heat it again when you add the egg and cream, that's when youwill finish cooking the veal).

When it's done, remove the meat and strain the broth over a fine mesh. Reserve3¼ cup of the stock for the velouté. Clean out the pan and place the meat and onions with the glaze in it. Cover (you can do this the day before too, but I thinkveal is best the day it is cooked — you can do the rest of the recipe earlier in the day and heat it gently if you would like — Dr Lostpast reheated left-overs in themicrowave successfully too).

Melt 4 T butter slowly, then add the flour and stir it in — let it cook for a fewminutes but do not let it brown. Slowly add the stock, whisking. Add vermouth and cognac. Cook it over medium heat for 10 minutes, stirring regularly. Addthe sliced mushrooms tossed in the lemon juice and cook for another 10 minutes or until the mushrooms are soft. This cooking is what helps give the sauce thebeautiful texture… don't rush it.

Remove 1 cup of the sauce without the mushrooms. Whisk the egg yolks andcream together and add the reserved hot velouté.

Add this to the meat and onions and cook over a low heat, stirring gently. Donot let it boil. Keep the sauce below 180° or the egg will curdle (using a wide-mouthed casserole makes this easy). Just for the heck of it I checked thetemperature of the veal cubes — they seemed to be around 145° — perfectmedium.

When everything is heated though taste for seasoning and add salt and pepper ifneeded, serve with noodles, rice or potatoes. Sprinkle with parsley and celery tops (I love the flavor of celery tops, originally, they were what was used and the bottoms were tossed!).

Sole Meunière

Ingredients

1/4 teaspoon kosher salt
1/4 cup all-purpose flour
4 sole fillets, (4 ounces each)
1/4 teaspoon freshly ground black pepper
2 teaspoons fresh lemon juice
4 tbsp unsalted butter
1 teaspoon minced flat-leaf parsley

Directions:

Combine flour, salt, and pepper. Dredge each fish fillet in the flourmixture until well coated.
In a large skillet over medium heat, melt 1 tablespoon of the butter.
Add the fish and brown about 3 minutes on each side, depending onthickness.
Transfer the fish to a platter and tent with foil. Add the remaining
butter to pan and turn up the heat to medium-high.
When the butter starts to brown, about 3 minutes, add the lemon juice
and parsley. Pour the butter over the fish and serve immediately.

Hachis Parmentier

Ingredients

3 garlic cloves, minced (or pressed)
2 onions, chopped
2 tablespoons olive oil
1 tablespoon butter
1 1/2 lbs lean ground beef
3 tomatoes, chopped
salt & pepper, to taste
1 tablespoon herbes de provence (or other herbs to your taste)
2 tablespoons parmesan cheese
1 egg yolk
3/4 cup gruyere cheese, grated (can also use emmental or similar)
4 -5 cups mashedr potatoes (instant is fine)

Directions

1. In a large frying pan, cook the onions & garlic in the butter & oliveoil on medium heat for about 5 minutes. Stir in the tomatoes, ground
beef, herbs, salt & pepper. Cook until the meat is browned thoroughly. Turn off heat & add egg yolk & Parmesan cheese, stirringto mix completely.

2. Spread the meat in the bottom of a lightly oiled oven proof dish (a9x13 would be perfect). Spread the potatoes on top of the meat

mixture. And finish by sprinkling the grated cheese on top.

3. Bake in 400 deg oven for 15 to 20 minutes, until the cheese is melted& the potatoes lightly browned.

Boudin Noir Aux Pommes

Ingredients

1 kg/ 2 pounds potatoes (cut in chunks)
12 slices of boudin noir sausage
1 onion or a handful of small onions (thinly sliced or halved if small
onions)
3-4 apples (peeled, cut in round slices)
Vegetable oil for frying
8 parsnips (peeled and thinly sliced – I used my food processor with a
special slicing blade)
Vinaigrette dressing:
25 g/ 2 tbsp butter for frying apples & onions
2 tsp grain mustard (or to your liking)
60 ml/ 1/4 cup olive oil
1 tsp salt
1 tbspXérès vinegar (or sherry/ red wine vinegar)
Pepper for seasoning

Method

1) Boil potatoes in a large pot of salted boiling water. Drain and setaside.

2) Prepare vinaigrette dressing. In a small bowl, mix olive oil, mustard, vinegar,salt and pepper. Mix well.

3) In a large heavy saucepan, fill oil no more than halfway and heat to 180°C/

39

350 F. You can test one slice of parsnip, drop it in the oil – if it starts sizzling,the oil is ready. Fry parsnip slices by batches, 2-3 minutes each, or until golden.
Set aside to drain on paper towels. Sprinkle with salt. Set aside.

4) In a frying pan, melt the butter, add onions and fry till golden for 3 minutes.
Add the apples, and continue frying 3 minutes on both sides, until golden. Setonions and apples aside.

5) In the same frying pan, add the boudin noir and fry on a medium heat for 2minutes on each sides. Slice potatoes, toss in the onions and vinaigrette.

6) Start with placing the potato salad on a plate. Place three slices of apples,followed by three slices of boudin noir on top. Sprinkle a generous amount of
parsnip crisps on top. Serve immediately while salad is warm.

Cheese Soufflé

Ingredients

1 cup whole milk
2 tablespoons finely grated Parmesan cheese
3 tablespoons unbleached all purpose flour
2 1/2 tablespoons unsalted butter
1/2 teaspoon salt
1/2 teaspoon paprika
4 large egg yolks
1 pinch of ground nutmeg
1 cup (packed) coarsely grated Gruyère cheese (about 4 ounces)
5 large egg whites

Preparation

Position rack in lower third of oven and preheat to 400°F. Butter 6-cup (11/2-quart) soufflé dish. Add Parmesan cheese and tilt dish,coating bottom and sides. Warm milk in heavy small saucepan over
medium-low heat until steaming.

Meanwhile, melt butter in heavy large saucepan over medium heat.
Add flour and whisk until mixture begins to foam and loses raw taste,about 3 minutes (do not allow mixture to brown). Remove saucepanfrom heat; let stand 1 minute. Pour in warm milk, whisking until

smooth. Return to heat and cook, whisking constantly until very thick,2 to 3 minutes. Remove from heat; whisk in paprika, salt, andnutmeg.

Add egg yolks 1 at a time, whisking to blend after each addition.
Scrape soufflé base into large bowl. Cool to lukewarm. do ahead Canbe made 2 hours ahead. Cover and let stand at room temperature.

Using electric mixer, beat egg whites in another large bowl until stiffbut not dry. Fold 1/4 of whites into lukewarm or room temperaturesoufflé base to lighten. Fold in remaining whites in 2 additions while
gradually sprinkling in Gruyère cheese. Transfer batter to prepareddish.

Place dish in oven and immediately reduce oven temperature to375°F. Bake until soufflé is puffed and golden brown on top andcenter moves only slightly when dish is shaken gently, about 25minutes (do not open oven door during first 20 minutes). Serveimmediately.

Steak Tartare

Ingredients

2 teaspoons brined capers, drained and rinsed
3 medium oil-packed anchovy fillets (optional, adjust salt if added),
rinsed and minced
2 large egg yolks
3 teaspoons Dijon mustard
2 tablespoons finely chopped red onion
10 ounces USDA prime beef tenderloin, cut into small dice, covered,
and refrigerated
4 teaspoons olive oil
2 tablespoons finely chopped Italian parsley leaves
4 dashes Worcestershire sauce
3 dashes hot sauce (such as Tabasco)
3/4 teaspoon crushed chile flakes (optional)

Instructions

1. 1Combine anchovies (if using), capers, and mustard in a nonreactivebowl. Using a fork or the back of a spoon, mash Ingredients untilevenly combined; mix in egg yolks.
2. 2Use a rubber spatula to fold remaining Ingredients into mustardmixture until thoroughly combined. Season well with salt and freshlyground black pepper. Serve immediately with toast points or french
fries.

Pot-au-feu

Ingredients

Brine

1/4 cup sugar

1/2 cup kosher salt

1 teaspoon whole black peppercorns

1 head of garlic, halved crosswise

2 pounds beef brisket

2 fresh bay leaves (or 1 dried)

3 4' pieces bone-in beef short ribs

Bouquet Garni, Meats, and Vegetables

10 sprigs flat-leaf parsley

1 head of garlic, halved crosswise

3 fresh bay leaves (or 1 dried)

10 sprigs thyme

1 teaspoon whole black peppercorns

3 whole cloves

2 pounds oxtails

3 2'–3'-long marrow bones

1 pound veal bones

2 pounds beef bones

*5 large carrots (about 1 lb.), peeled (2 chopped, 3 cut into 2'
pieces)*

1 pound veal breast

1 onion, quartered

2 celery stalks, chopped

2 rutabagas (about 1 lb.), peeled, cut into wedges

1 1-lb. piece garlic sausage

44

1 pound baby potatoes
1 small head of savoy cabbage (about 1 lb.), halved
Sauces and Garnishes
1/4 cup finely chopped flat-leaf parsley
1/2 cup extra-virgin olive oil
1/4 cup finely chopped fresh tarragon
1/4 cup finely chopped fresh chives
Kosher salt and freshly ground black pepper
2 garlic cloves, minced
2 tablespoons prepared white horseradish, drained
1/4 cup crème fraîche
Dijon mustard
Whole grain mustard
Toasted sliced country bread

Preparation
Brine
Bring first 5 Ingredients and 8 cups water to a simmer in a mediumsaucepan over medium heat, stirring until sugar and salt dissolve.
Remove from heat; let cool to room temperature. Place brisket andshort ribs in a large baking dish. Pour brine over to cover completely.
Cover and chill for at least 8 hours or overnight. Remove meat; rinseand set aside.
Bouquet Garni, Meats, and Vegetables
Place first 6 Ingredients in center of a triple layer of cheesecloth.

Gather up edges; tie with kitchen twine to form a bundle for bouquetgarni. Wrap marrow bones in cheesecloth; tie into a bundle withtwine. If desired, tie oxtails with twine around circumference to keep
meat from falling off bones.

Place brisket, short ribs, bouquet garni, marrow bones, oxtails, beefbones, veal bones, veal breast, 2 chopped carrots, celery, and onion in
a very large heavy pot. Add water to cover meat (about 7 qt.). Bringto a boil, skimming off any scum and fat that rise to the surface.
Reduce heat and simmer, skimming occasionally, until short ribs aretender, 2–2 1/2 hours.
Transfer short ribs to a 13x9x2" baking dish; add 4 cups broth frompot and tent with foil to keep meat warm and moist. Add sausage to
pot; continue simmering until sausage is cooked through and remaining meats are tender, about 30 minutes longer.
Transfersausage, brisket, oxtails, and marrow bones to dish with short ribs.
Place a large strainer over another large pot; strain broth, discardingremaining meats, bones, and other solids in strainer. (You should
have about 10 cups broth.) Return broth to a boil; add rutabagas,cabbage, potatoes, and 2" pieces of carrots. Simmer until vegetables
are tender but not mushy, about 30 minutes.

Sauces and Garnishes

Mix first 5 Ingredients in a small bowl to make salsa verde. Seasonwith salt and pepper; set aside. Stir crème fraîche and horseradish in
another small bowl; season with salt.
Transfer vegetables to a platter. Thinly slice brisket against the grain;cut sausage into 2" pieces. Return meats to baking dish.
Season broth in pot to taste with salt and pepper; divide among bowls.
(Reserve broth from meats for another use.) Serve meats and vegetables with salsa verde, horseradish crème fraîche, and bothmustards in small bowls alongside. Serve with toasted country bread.

Basque Piperade

Ingredients

1 pint pureed san marzano tomatoes (optional)
1 quart can whole peeled san marzano tomatoes
10-15 cloves fresh sliced garlic
1 jar/4-6 whole roasted sweet red bell peppers
3-4 large eggs
1.5 whole yellow onions, julienned
1 tspchili powder
2 tsp smoked spanish paprika
1 tsp kosher salt
2 bay leaves
1 tsp sugar (optional)
1 tsp fresh cracked black pepper
6-8 slices of crusty bread, brushed with olive oil
1 cup olive oil

Preparation

Preheat oven to 450°
Prep chop your onions, garlic and red peppers.
Sauté the onions and sliced garlic in olive oil on medium
high heatuntil translucent (5-7 minutes).
Add your spices and "bloom" them out (sauté until you start
to smellthem)
Add your can of tomatoes. Break them up a bit with a metal
spoon,then add roasted red peppers to the party.
Add bay leaves and season to taste with salt and pepper

Turn heat down to low and simmer for 25-30 minutes. Adjustseasoning if needed.

Place about 2 cups of the finished product in an oven-proof cast ironpan (a small paella pan works great)

Make resting places for your eggs with a spoon and crack one egginto each of those spots.(crack into a bowl first to help with pouringand to avoid the risk of a cracked shell falling into the stew)

Bake for 7-10 minutes, until the egg whites begin to set, but the yolkremains runny.

Slice and grill bread and serve with dish.

Magret de Canard

Ingredients

2 peaches (peeled and sliced)
2 large duck breasts
6 garlic cloves (sliced fine)
5 large potatoes
1 tbsp butter
2 handfuls of chopped parsley
Salt & Pepper

Method

Preheat the oven on 180° celsius.
Just before you start cooking the duck, start frying on a medium heat the sliced
potatoes with one tbsp butter for 8 minutes. Set aside.
In a large cool frying pan, place your 2 duck breasts skin touching the base.
Switch on the heat to moderate and start frying. Every 5 minutes or so, when the
duck fat melts, pour in a bowl, reserve the fat, and continue frying. Too much oilwill make your duck skin burn.
Pour 8 tbps (or more if you wish and according to your taste) of the reservedduck fat onto the potatoes and continue frying till cooked and golden. You'd be
surprised at how fast it cooks with duck fat. Flip potatoes constantly. Add salt.

By 20-25 minutes they should be cooked. Put potatoes in a small cake mold andpress gently with a potato masher or a large spoon so the potatoes take a good
shape. You don't want to mash the potatoes, just press them. Place in the ovenfor 5-8 minutes.
After 20-25 minutes of duck frying, flip over the breasts and cook maximum 5minutes depending on how you like your 'cuisson' (2 mins if you like the breast
rosé/pink). Meanwhile you can fry the garlic in a tsp of duck fat until golden andthe sliced peach for 3 minutes. They can be fried in the same pan.
Take the potato cake out of the oven, remove from mold and place on a serving
plate. Put the chopped parsley and fried garlic on top. Slice the duck breast, season with salt and pepper. Serve immediately.

Garbure

Ingredients

1 Spanish onion, diced
4 oz. pancetta, cut into ½" cubes
4 precooked confit duck legs
4 garlic cloves, crushed
1 small head of savoy cabbage (1½–2 lb.), core removed, sliced into
1" x 3" strips
3½ quarts unsalted chicken stock
3 stalks celery, diced
2 carrots, peeled and cut into ¼" slices
½ lb. Yukon Gold potatoes, peeled and cut into 1" cubes
1 medium-size leek (tough outer leaves removed), sliced into
¼" pieces
A bouquet garni comprising 1 piece of leek (3" x 3"), 3 thyme sprigs,
1 rosemary sprig, 1 bay leaf, 3 parsley stems, and 2 sage sprigs tied with kitchen string
1½ cups dried cannellini beans, soaked in water overnight, strained
Salt and pepper to taste

Directions

Heat a 6-quart Dutch oven over medium-high heat, add the pancetta, and cook,
stirring, for 4 minutes or until golden brown. Remove and set aside, keeping the

52

fat in the pot. Reduce heat to medium; add the diced onion and crushed garlic

cloves, and cook, stirring, for 8 minutes or until soft.

Pick the meat from the confit duck legs, discarding the skin and bones, and

shred. Incorporate the shredded duck meat with the onion-and-garlic mixture.

Add the chicken stock, cabbage, carrots, celery, leek, potatoes, cannellini beans,

and bouquet garni. Bring the soup to a simmer; then cook, stirring occasionally,

for 45 minutes or until the vegetables are tender.

Stir the reserved pancetta into the soup, remove the bouquet garni, season to

taste, and serve immediately.

Cassoulet

Ingredients

10 tbsp. duck fat or olive oil
1 lb. dried great northern beans
2 onions, chopped
16 cloves garlic, smashed
2 large ham hocks
2 carrots, chopped
1/2 lb. pancetta, cubed
1 lb. pork shoulder, cut into 1"cubes
4 sprigs thyme
4 sprigs oregano
1 cup whole peeled canned tomatoes
3 bay leaves
2 cups chicken broth
1 cup white wine
1 lb. pork sausages
4 confit duck legs (optional)
2 cups bread crumbs

Directions

1. Soak beans in a 4-qt. bowl in 7 1/2 cups water overnight. Heat 2tbsp. duck fat in a 6-qt. pot over medium-high heat. Add half the garlic, onions, and carrots and cook until lightly browned, about 10 minutes. Add ham hocks along with beans and their water and boil. Reduce heat and simmer beans until

tender, about 1 1/2 hours.

2. Transfer ham hocks to a plate; let cool. Pull off meat; discard skin, bone, and gristle. Chop meat; add to beans. Set aside.

3. Heat 2 tbsp. duck fat in a 5-qt. dutch oven over medium-high heat. Add pork and brown for 8 minutes. Add pancetta; cook for 5 minutes. Add remaining garlic, onions, and carrots; cook until lightly browned, about 10 minutes. Tietogether oregano, thyme, and bay leaves with twine; add to pan with tomatoes; cook until liquid thickens, 8–10 minutes. Add wine; reduce by half. Add broth;boil. Reduce heat to medium-low; cook, uncovered, until liquid has thickened, about 1 hour. Discard herbs; set dutch oven aside.

4. Meanwhile, sear duck legs in 2 tbsp. duck fat in a 12" skillet over medium-high heat for 8 minutes; transfer to a plate. Brown sausages in the fat, about 8 minutes. Cut sausages into 1/2" slices. Pull duck meat off bones. Discard fat andbones. Stir duck and sausages into pork stew.

5. Heat oven to 300˚. Mix beans and pork stew in a 4-qt. earthenware casserole. Cover with bread crumbs; drizzle with remaining duck fat. Bake, uncovered, for3 hours. Raise oven temperature to 500˚; cook cassoulet until crust is golden, about 5 minutes.

Pan-seared Foie Gras

Ingredients

*Coarse salt 1 whole duck foiegras, about 1 1/2 pounds,
slightly chilled 6 slices
white bread, cut in rounds Black pepper, freshly ground
4 fresh black mission figs, halved 1 tablespoon extra virgin
olive oil 6 tarragon
leaves, chopped
2 shallots, finely chopped
1 orange, juiced, divided
1/2 cup port wine
1 pat butter
2 tablespoons balsamic vinegar
1/2 teaspoon orange zest, grated Pinch sugar
1 bunch arugula
3 heads endive, julienned
1/2 lemon, juiced
1/2 bunch fresh chives, roughly chopped 1 tablespoon extra
virgin olive oil*

Directions

Carefully pull apart the 2 lobes of the foiegras with your
hands and remove the
veins that are lodged between them. Using a sharp knife
dipped in boiling water,
cut each lobe into 1-inch medallions, approximately 6 (4-
ounce) slices. Score the

top of each medallion in a diamond pattern and season with salt and pepper. Searthe medallions in a hot, dry pan for 30 seconds per side, seasoned side down

first. Remove to a warmed platter lined with paper towels to drain.

Lower heat to medium and pour out a bit of the rendered duck fat. Fry the breadrounds until brown, about 2 minutes each side, set aside. Wipe out the pan and

coat with olive oil. Brown the figs, cut side down, then add the shallots andtarragon. Cook for 2 minutes. Deglaze the pan with port, juice of 1/2 orange and

balsamic vinegar, cook down, about 3 minutes. Finish off the sauce with butter,a pinch of sugar, orange zest, salt and pepper.

Combine the endive, arugula and chives together in a small bowl. Toss withremaining orange juice, lemon juice and olive oil, season with salt and pepper.

Arrange a handful of salad on each plate and lay the toast on top. Carefully placea foiegras medallion on each toast round. Top with figs, drizzle with port wine

sauce. Garnish with chives and serve at once.

Confit de Canard

Ingredients

1/3 cup Kosher salt (about 4 teaspoons per pound of duck, half for short
preserving periods)
2 fatty ducks (or 4 sets of thighs and drumsticks)
3tablespoons parsley,
minced 4 shallots,
minced 1 bay leaf,
crumbled ½ teaspoon thyme leaves,
crumbled 2 quarts rendered poultry and pork fat 2
teaspoons white peppercorns, crushed 2 cups pork lard for
storing the confit(only if there is not enough duck fat) 1
garlic head, halved and stuck with 2cloves

Directions

Quarter the ducks and remove the backbones. Cut and trim off as much fat aspossible. Grind any excess skin and all the fat in a food processor, place in a
deep saucepan with 1 cup water and render the fat (simmer it over low heat forabout 45 minutes, uncovered), strain, and reserve.
Cut each breast into halves with the wings attached. Roll each piece of duck inthe salt and place it in a large stainless glass or earthen bowl. Sprinkle each piece of duck with a mixture of the shallots, herbs, and spices and scatter any

remaining salt over the top. Cover loosely and refrigerate 24 hours.

NOTE:

Thismay be cut down to a few hours if it is to be eaten within a week or two.

Rinse quickly, then wipe the pieces of duck to remove all the salt, herbs, spices,and liquid.

Heat the strained fat in a deep, wide kettle. Add the duck, 1/2 cup of water, thehalved garlic head, and enough rendered poultry or pork fat to cover. Bring the mixture to a boil. Lower heat and cook at a simmer for 1 1/2 hours, or until theduck flesh can be easily pierced with a straw. Do not let the mixture boil.

Remove the duck, drain and discard any loose bones. Strain the warmed fat. Putabout 1 cup of warmed fat into each of the bowls or mason jars intended for storage of the confit and cool in order to congeal the fat. Arrange the duck pieces in the containers without compacting them. Strain the remaining fat, tepid but not hot, over the duck to cover. The pieces of duck must be completely submerged in the fat. Cover and chill until solid. Cover with a layer of melted lard. Cover tightly with a glass top or with plastic wrap and store in a cool place such as a cold cellar or the refrigerator. Leave to ripen at least 1 month. It keeps well for 6 months.

To use the confit, set the jars or bowl in a warm oven. When the fat softens,remove pieces desired. Return jar or bowl to the refrigerator. Be sure all of the
remaining pieces are covered with fat. The duck can be served at roomtemperature or warmed in an oven, then Sauteed to crisp the skin.

PouletBasquaise

Ingredients

2 chicken legs (drumstick+tigh), skin on
2 tsp olive oil
2 garlic cloves, minced
1 onion, chopped
2 red bell pepper, peeled and cubed
1/4 cup white wine
1/4 tsp paprika
1 14-ounce can crushed tomatoes
Salt and pepper to taste
1/2 tsp thyme

Directions

1. In a deep saucepan, heat olive oil on medium heat. Brown chicken forabout 8 minutes. Remove from pan and set aside. Drain excess fat ifneeded.

2. Add onion and garlic and cook for 1 minutes, paying attention not toburn them.

3. Deglaze with wine and scrub the bottom of the pan with a woodenspoon or spatula.

4. Add bell pepper, tomato, paprika, thyme, salt and pepper. Mix andreturn chicken to the pan.

5. Reduce heat, cover with a lid and simmer until chicken is cookedthrough, about 30 minutes. Serve with rice on the side, and you'regood to go!

Lamprey à la Bordelaise

Ingredients
1,500kg of soft leeks
1 lamprey of 1,200kg
6 pickling onions
6 petitsoignons
6 cloves of garlic
6 shallots
1 bouquet garni
300g of ham
2 cloves
15cl of oil of olive and groundnut
7cl of cognac or armagnac
1 bottle of wine from the Côtes de Bourg appelation (red)
Salt and pepper
1 soupspoon of caster sugar
1 soupspoon of flour

Directions
Attach the lamprey by the head, make a section for the tail
and collect the blood.
Warm the fish in some boiling water and remove the central
cordon, cut the head
and the tail. Cut the lamprey in sections and make it
marinade 3 or 4 hours in the
red wine. Cook it in a mixture of olive oil and groundnut,
slice thinly shallots,

pickling onions and thinly cut ham. After a moment, add the crushed garlic, theflour, and the marinade. Put down the bouquet garni, add salt and pepper.

Let simmer slowly during one hour. Make sweat the leeks. Then cut them inbatonnets of 10 centimeters and put them into the sauce. Cook the lamprey.

Make it burn with the chosen alcohol and put them down in the frying pan.

Sweeten, prolong the cooking on very soft fire even one hour. Bind the saucewith the blood of the lamprey.

Let cook for 10 minutes more.

Quenelles of Pike with Lobster Sauce

Ingredients
For the quenelle base:
12,5 cl milk
60 g flour
30 g butter
1 egg For the forcemeat:
300 g pike-perch, filleted and skinned
50 cl well-chilled double cream
pepper
grated nutmeg 2 egg whites
2 teaspoons salt
For the lobster sauce:
2 lobster heads or 6 scampi heads 1 medium onion
1 medium carrot
2 cloves garlic, peeled
1 sprig fresh thyme
50 g tomato concentrate
35 cl Cognac
25 cl olive oil
75 cl double cream
2 or 3 soupspoons NoillyPrat
5 cl white wine
Salt and pepper Poaching liquid for the quenelles:
1 l fish stock

Directions

Prepare the quenelle base first. Cut the butter into large cubes. Pour the milk into

a saucepan, add the butter, and bring to a boil. Add the flour, then continuecooking on low heat and mixing thoroughly for 3 or 4 minutes. Remove the

saucepan from the heat, add the egg and mix well. Set the mixture aside to coolcompletely.

Then make the fish forcemeat. Rinse the fish under cold running water. Place it

on a cutting board and chop it finely, using a large knife. Put the chopped fishinto a large bowl and mix in the salt, 1 pinch pepper, and 1 pinch nutmeg. Put

the fish forcemeat and quenelle base into a food processor together. Blend for 3 -4 minutes. Add the egg whites and blend again. Add 3/4 of the cream and keep

the rest of the cream chilled. Blend the mixture until the consistency is perfectly

smooth. Gently mix in the rest of the cream, using a spatula. Let the mixture restin the refrigerator for at least 1 hour 30 minutes.

Prepare the sauce. Peel the onion. Peel and wash the carrot. Cut the onion andcarrot into large cubes. Heat the olive oil in a large saucepan. Add the seafood

heads and crush them with a pestle. Add the onion, carrot, garlic, thyme, andtomato concentrate. Add the Cognac and white wine. Add just enough water to

cover. Bring to a boil and simmer to reduce the volume

by three-quarters (at least 30 minutes). Add the cream. Reduce the volume by
another quarter on low heat. Strain the sauce through a fine sieve or conicalstrainer, pressing it through with the back of a spoon. Add salt and pepper totaste.

Take the forcemeat out of the refrigerator. Prepare a dish and a small saucepanof boiling water. Dip two spoons in boiling water, scoop up some mixture with
one spoon, heaping it up well, then use the other spoon to compact and shape thequenelle. Then use that spoon to remove the quenelle from the first spoon.

Transfer the quenelle from one spoon to the other several times to give it an evenshape and lay it gently in the dish. Dip the spoons in the boiling water between
each quenelle.

Heat the fish stock in a saucepan (do not let it boil), then reduce to low heat.

Drop the quenelles gently into the stock and simmer for 8 minutes. Use askimmer to turn the quenelles over and simmer for another 8 minutes on lowheat.

Heat up the sauce in a saucepan. Add the NoillyPrat. Arrange the quenelles on
an ovenproof dish, pour the sauce over them, and heat under the grill for 2minutes just before serving.

The quenelles may be cooked in advance, but should be reheated in simmering
fish stock at the last minute. If you are unable to prepare lobster sauce, thequenelles may be served with a white-wine sauce.

Gigot D'AgneauPleureur

Ingredients

*1 large red capsicum, thickly sliced 4 medium sebago
potatoes, cut into 4cm
pieces 1 large eggplant, cut into 4cm pieces 1 large green
capsicum, thickly
sliced 1 bulb garlic, halved crossways
2 tablespoons olive oil
1 1/2 tablespoons lemon juice
1/3 cup mint jelly, warmed
8 lamb loin chops, trimmed
1 tablespoon fresh thyme leaves*

Method

Preheat oven to 200°C/180°C fan-forced. Place potato,
capsicum and eggplantin a large roasting pan. Drizzle with 1
1/2 tablespoons oil. Toss to combine. Add
garlic to pan. Roast for 45 minutes.
Meanwhile, combine mint jelly, lemon juice and thyme in a
bowl. Heatremaining oil in a large non-stick frying pan over
medium-high heat. Add lamb.
Cook for 2 minutes each side or until browned. Remove
from heat. Brush both
sides of lamb with half the mint jelly mixture.

Arrange lamb over vegetables. Season with salt and pepper.
Roast for a further

20 to 25 minutes, brushing with remaining mint jelly
mixture halfway through
cooking, for medium or until cooked to your liking. Serve.

Bouillabaisse

Ingredients

Rouille

3 tablespoons water

One 3-inch piece of baguette, cut into 1/2-inch dice

1/2 teaspoon cayenne pepper

2 garlic cloves

3 tablespoons extra-virgin olive oil

1/2 teaspoon kosher salt

Bouillabaisse

2 leeks, white and light green parts only, thinly sliced

3 tablespoons extra-virgin olive oil, plus more for drizzling

1 fennel bulb—fronds reserved, bulb cored and cut into 1/4-inch dice

1 onion, cut into 1/4-inch dice

2 tomatoes, cut into 1/2-inch dice

4 garlic cloves, 3 coarsely chopped

Pinch of saffron threads

2 bay leaves

5 cups store-bought fish stock

2 tablespoons pastis or Pernod

Eight 1/2-inch-thick baguette slices, cut on the bias

One 2-pound live lobster

1/4 teaspoon cayenne pepper

3 Yukon Gold potatoes (1 1/2 pounds), peeled and cut into 1/2-inch dice

1 pound monkfish, cut into sixteen 1 1/2-inch pieces
2 dozen littleneck clams, scrubbed
1 pound skinless halibut fillet, cut into sixteen 1 1/2-inch
pieces
1 pound skinless red snapper fillets, cut into sixteen 1 1/2-
inch
pieces

Preparation

In a mini food processor, sprinkle the diced bread with the
water and let stand until the water is absorbed,
about 5 minutes. Add the garlic, cayenne and salt and
process until the bread and garlic are coarsely
chopped. With the machine on, drizzle in the olive oil and
process until the rouille is smooth. Transfer to a
bowl and refrigerate.
In a very large, deep skillet, heat the 3 tablespoons of olive
oil. Add the leeks, onion, fennel and chopped
garlic and cook over moderate heat until translucent, about 5
minutes. Add the tomatoes and cook until they
begin to break down, about 5 minutes. Add the bay leaves,
saffron and pastis and bring to a boil. Add the
fish stock and bring to a simmer. Cook over low heat until
the vegetables are very tender, about 20 minutes.
Discard the bay leaves.
In a food processor, pulse the vegetables and broth to a
coarse puree. Strain through a fine sieve set over
the skillet.

Bring a large pot of water to a boil. Add the lobster and cook until it turns bright red, about 4 minutes.

Drain and rinse the lobster under cold water until cool enough to handle. Remove the tail, claw and knuckle meat and cut into 1-inch pieces.

Preheat the broiler. Arrange the baguette slices on a baking sheet and broil them 6 inches from the heat for about 1 minute per side, until the slices are golden brown around the edges. Rub each slice with the remaining whole garlic clove and drizzle lightly with olive oil.

Add the potatoes and cayenne pepper to the broth and bring to a simmer. Cook over moderately high heat until the potatoes are just tender, about 10 minutes; season with salt and pepper. Add the clams, cover and cook over moderate heat until they just begin to open, about 3 minutes. Add the monkfish, cover and simmer for 2 minutes. Add the lobster, snapper and halibut, cover and simmer until the clams are open and all the fish is cooked through, about 4 minutes.

Set a baguette toast in each of 8 shallow bowls. Ladle the fish and broth over the toasts and top each serving with 1 tablespoon of the rouille. Sprinkle with fennel fronds and serve immediately.

Pissaladière

Ingredients

1 tablespoon olive oil
50g butter
2 cloves garlic, crushed
3 large onions (600g), peeled and sliced thinly
1 sprig fresh thyme
1 bay leaf
3/4 cup (110g) self-raising flour
1 tablespoon baby capers, rinsed
30g butter, extra
3/4 cup (11g) plain flour
20 drained anchovy fillets, halved lengthways
3/4 cup (180ml) buttermilk
1/2 cup (90g) small seeded black olives

Preparation

Heat the butter and oil in a large saucepan over low heat and add the onions,garlic, bay leaf and thyme. Cover the pot and let the mixture cook gently forabout 30 minutes, stirring occasionally. You want the onions to be soft but not browned.
Let the mixture cook uncovered for a further 10 minutes. Remove the bay leafand thyme, and stir in the capers.
Preheat the oven to 220°C and oil an oven tray.
Make the base by sifting the flours into a large bowl. Rub in the extra butter, and

then stir in the buttermilk to form a soft dough (mine needed more flour). Turnthe dough on to a lightly floured surface and knead until it is smooth.

Roll the dough into a rectangular shape that is about 25cm x 35cm. Place on tothe tray.

Spread the onion mixture over the dough, up to the edges. Top with the anchovyfillets, placing them in a diamond pattern. Put an olive in the middle of each diamond.

Bake for about 30 minutes, or until the base is crisp.

Ratatouille

Ingredients

1 tbsp. dried herbes de Provence
1/2 cup extra-virgin olive oil
2 large yellow onions, quartered
6 cloves garlic, smashed and peeled
2 medium zucchini (about 1 1/4 lbs.), cut into 2" pieces
1 bay leaf
1 red bell pepper, stemmed, seeded, and quartered
1 medium eggplant (about 14 oz.), cut into 2" pieces
10 whole peeled tomatoes from the can, drained
1 yellow bell pepper, stemmed, seeded, and quartered
1 tbsp. chopped fresh basil leaves
Kosher salt and freshly ground black pepper, to taste
1 tbsp. chopped fresh flat-leaf parsley

Instructions

1. Heat oven to 400°. Heat oil in a 6-qt. Dutch oven over medium heat. Add herbes de Provence, garlic, onions, and bay leaf; cover and cook, stirring occasionally, until soft and fragrant, about 10 minutes.

2. Increase heat to high; stir in the zucchini, eggplant, peppers, and tomatoes and season with salt and pepper. Uncover pot, transfer to the oven, and bake, stirring occasionally, until vegetables are tender and lightly browned, about 1 1/2 hours.

3. Stir in basil and parsley, transfer ratatouille to a serving bowl, and serve warm or at room temperature.

Roasted Chicken and Garlic

Ingredients

1 whole chicken (3 1/2 to 4 pounds), rinsed and patted dry (giblets
removed)
40 garlic cloves (3 to 4 heads), unpeeled
Coarse salt and ground pepper
2 tablespoons butter, room temperature
6 sprigs fresh thyme

Directions

1. Preheat oven to 475 degrees. Place garlic in a medium bowl; coverwith another same-size bowl, creating a dome. Hold bowls togethertightly, and shake vigorously until skins are loosened, about 30 seconds. Remove and discard skins; set garlic aside.

2. Place chicken in a large ovenproof skillet or roasting pan. Rub allover with 1 tablespoon butter; season with salt and pepper. Addthyme, garlic, and remaining tablespoon butter to skillet.

3. Roast, basting occasionally with juices and stirring garlic, until aninstant-read thermometer inserted in thickest part of a thigh (avoidingbone) registers 165 degrees, 45 to 60 minutes. Transfer to a platter, and let rest 10 minutes. Carve chicken, and serve with garlic and panjuices.

NavarinD'Agneau (Navarin oflamb)

Ingredients

*2 x 1kg boned rolled lamb shoulders, fat trimmed, cut into 4cm pieces 2
tablespoons olive oil
2 tablespoons tomato paste
2 tablespoons plain flour
750ml (3 cups) Campbell's Real Stock Chicken 3 garlic
cloves, crushed
6 fresh thyme sprigs
250ml (1 cup) dry white wine
16 (about 950g) chat (baby coliban) potatoes, halved 3 dried
bay leaves
2 bunches spring onions, ends trimmed 2 bunches baby
(Dutch) carrots, ends
trimmed, peeled 230g (1 1/2 cups) frozen green peas 300g
green beans, topped
Crusty bread, to serve*

Method

1. Step 1 - Heat the oil in a large stockpot over medium-high heat. Add athird of the lamb and cook, turning, for 3-4 minutes or until brown.
   Transfer to a plate. Repeat, in 2 more batches, with the remaininglamb, reheating the pan between batches.
2. Step 2 - Add the flour, tomato paste and garlic and cook, stirring, for

2 minutes. Remove from heat and whisk in the stock and wine. Addthe thyme and bay leaves and bring to the boil over high heat. Return
lamb to pan. Reduce heat to low and simmer, covered, stirringoccasionally, for 1 hour 10 minutes.

3. Step 3 - Add the potato to the lamb mixture and cook, covered, for 30minutes. Uncover and cook, stirring occasionally, for 10 minutes or
until sauce thickens.

4. Step 4 - Meanwhile, cook the carrots in a large saucepan of boilingwater for 3-4 minutes or until tender. Transfer to a plate. Repeat withthe spring onions and the beans.

5. Step 5 - Add the carrots, onions, beans and peas to the lamb mixtureand cook for 2-3 minutes or until heated through. Taste and season
with salt and pepper. 6. Place the lamb mixture in a large serving dishand serve immediately with crusty bread if desired.

Foie de Veau à la Lyonnaise

Ingredients

2 tbsp. grapeseed oil
1 russet potato, peeled, cut into ⅛'"-thick batons, and soaked inwater
2 cloves garlic (1 smashed and 1 minced)
6 tbsp. unsalted butter
4 slices bacon, roughly chopped
Kosher salt and freshly ground black pepper, to taste
½ cup flour
2 lbs. veal or beef liver, trimmed
1 tbsp. fresh lemon juice
¼ cup clarified butter
Fleur de sel, to taste
½ cup minced flat-leaf parsley

Instructions

1. Drain potatoes and pat dry with paper towels. Heat oil in a 12" skillet over medium-high heat. Add potatoes and cook, turning occasionally, until light brown. Add 2 tbsp. unsalted butter and smashed garlic and season with salt and pepper. Cook, spooning butter over potatoes, until golden brown and tender, about 5 minutes more. Transfer potatoes to a plate; set aside. Wipe out skillet.

2. Return skillet to medium heat. Add bacon and cook, stirring occasionally, until browned and crisp, about 12 minutes. Using a slotted spoon, transfer bacon to paper

towels and wipe out skillet.

3. Using a sharp knife, slice liver horizontally into 4 thin slices. Season liver with salt and pepper. Put flour on a plate and dredge liver in flour; transfer to a rack set inside a baking sheet. Heat 2 tbsp. clarified butter in reserved skillet over medium-high heat. Add 2 slices liver and cook until browned, about 2 minutes. Flip liver, add 2 tbsp. unsalted butter, and cook to desired temperature, about 1 minute more for medium rare. Transfer liver to paper towels and repeat with remaining clarified butter, liver, and unsalted butter. add lemon juice to pan, along with parsley and remaining garlic. Stir to combine. To serve divide potatoes between

4 serving plates. Top potatoes with liver and garnish with bacon. Spoon pan sauce over liver and sprinkle with fleur de sel.

Aligot

Ingredients

1 pound Yukon Gold or other all-purpose potatoes, peeled and cut
into large chunks
4 tablespoons unsalted butter
2 ounces Langres cheese
2 ounces Monte Enebro cheese
Coarse salt and freshly ground black pepper
1/2 cup milk, warmed
White truffle oil, for serving
Toasted baguette slices, for serving

Directions

1. Place potatoes in a large saucepan and add enough water to cover;generously salt water and bring to a boil, adjusting the heat so that thewater is bubbling, but not too rapidly. Cook until potatoes are tender, about 20 minutes.

2. Drain and mash or pass potatoes through a ricer into saucepan. Placeover low heat and add milk; stir to combine. Add butter and stir until melted. Beat with a wooden spoon until stringy.

3. Remove from heat and stir in cheeses until melted; season with saltand pepper. Transfer to a bowl and drizzle with truffle oil. Serve withtoasts.

Fondue Savoyarde

Ingredients

1 clove garlic, peeled and crushed
1 1/2 cups Savoyard white wine, or other light, dry
white wine
1 lb. beaufort or gruyère cheese, grated or cubed
1 tsp. freshly grated nutmeg
Freshly ground black pepper
1/4 cup kirsch
8 slices French country bread, cut into 1" cubes,
each one with a piece of crust

Directions

1. Rub a medium heavy pot with garlic; discard garlic. Add wine and bring to aboil over high heat. Reduce heat to medium and gradually add cheese, stirring constantly with a wooden spoon, until cheese has melted. Do not boil. Continueto cook, stirring frequently, until mixture has thickened, about 20 minutes. Add nutmeg, pepper to taste, and kirsch. Transfer fondue to a chafing dish or fonduepot.
2. Serve with bread cubes and fondue forks. Stir frequently. If fondue becomes too thick, stir in 1/4 cup of dry white wine.

Tartiflette

Ingredients
2 1/2 lb potatoes, peeled
1/2 lb slab bacon, cut in small dice
1 medium onion, thinly sliced
3/4 cup dry white wine
1 lbReblochon-style cheese, sliced
Salt
Pepper

Directions
1. Preheat the oven to 350 F. Place the potatoes in the pot, cover withwater, and bring to a boil. Cook for about 20 minutes, or until thepotatoes are easily pierced with the knife. Remove from the heat, drain, and let sit until they are cool enough to handle. Cut the potatoesinto small dice and set aside.

2. In the sauté pan, cook the bacon over high heat until browned. Drain,leaving 1 tablespoon of fat in the skillet and add the onion. Cook over moderately high heat for about 5 minutes until golden brown then addthe bacon and wine and cook for another 5 minutes, stirringoccasionally. Add the potatoes and season with salt and pepper.

3. Remove the potato mixture from the heat and place half of it in theovenproof dish. Spread half the cheese slices atop the potato mixture.

Cover this with the other half of the potato mixture. Top with theremainder of the cheese. Bake in the hot oven for 20 minutes, or until
golden brown and bubbling. Serve hot.

Gratin Dauphinois (Potato Gratin)

Ingredients

*500 ml (2 cups) milk (whole or part-skim, not skim; I don't
recommend using non-dairy milk as the
dish turns out watery)
1 kg (2.2 pounds) potatoes, a mix of waxy and baking
potatoes (if you prefer to use only one type,
pick waxy potatoes, not too firm)
freshly grated nutmeg
1 1/2 teaspoons salt
3 tablespoons finely chopped chives (optional)
1 clove garlic, sliced lengthwise
60 ml (1/4 cup) heavy cream (use whipping cream in the UK
and crème fraîcheliquide in France)*

Instructions

1. Peel the potatoes, rinse them briefly, and slice them thinly (about3mm or 1/10th of an inch) and evenly. (A food processor or amandoline come in handy at this point.) Do not rinse after slicing, or
you will lose all that precious starch.
2. Combine the sliced potatoes, milk, salt and a good grating of nutmegin a saucepan. Bring to a simmer over medium-low heat, and keep
simmering for 8 minutes, stirring the potatoes and scraping thebottom of the pan regularly to prevent sticking/scorching. The milk
will gradually thicken to a creamy consistency.

3. While the potatoes are simmering, preheat the oven to 220°C (430°F)and rub the bottom and sides of a medium earthenware or glassbaking dish (I use an oval dish that's 26 cm/10 inches at its widest,
and 2 liters/2 quarts in capacity) with the cut sides of the garlic clove.

4. Transfer half of the potatoes into the baking dish, sprinkle with thechives if using, and drizzle with half of the cream. Add the rest of thepotatoes, pour the cooking milk over them, and drizzle with theremaining cream.

5. Bake for 35 to 40 minutes, until bubbly on the edges and nicelybrowned at the top. Let stand for about 10 minutes before serving.

Chef Marino

Coq au Vin

Ingredients

A heavy, 10-inch, fireproof casserole
A 3-to 4-ounce chunk of bacon
2 1/2 to 3 pounds cut-up frying chicken
2 tablespoons butter
1/8 teaspoon pepper
1/2 teaspoon salt
3 cups young, full-bodied red wine such as Burgundy,
Beaujolais, Cotes du Rhone or
Chianti
1/4 cup cognac
1/2 tablespoon tomato paste
1 to 2 cups brown chicken stock, brown stock
or canned beef bouillon
1/4 teaspoon thyme
2 cloves mashed garlic
12 to 24 brown-braised onions (recipe follows)
1 bay leaf
Salt and pepper
1/2 pound sautéed mushrooms (recipe follows)
2 tablespoons softened butter
3 tablespoons flour
Sprigs of fresh parsley

Directions

1. Remove the rind of and cut the bacon into lardons
(rectangles 1/4-inch across

and 1 inch long). Simmer for 10 minutes in 2 quarts of water. Rinse in coldwater. Dry. [Deb note: As noted, I'd totally skip this step next time.]

2. Sauté the bacon slowly in hot butter until it is very lightly browned. Removeto a side dish.

3. Dry the chicken thoroughly. Brown it in the hot fat in the casserole.

4. Season the chicken. Return the bacon to the casserole with the chicken. Coverand cook slowly for 10 minutes, turning the chicken once.

5. Uncover, and pour in the cognac. Averting your face, ignite the cognac with alighted match. Shake the casserole back and forth for several seconds until the flames subside.

6. Pour the wine into the casserole. Add just enough stock or bouillon to coverthe chicken. Stir in the tomato paste, garlic and herbs. Bring to the simmer.

Cover and simmer slowly for 25 to 30 minutes, or until the chicken is tender andits juices run a clear yellow when the meat is pricked with a fork. Remove the chicken to a side dish.

7. While the chicken is cooking, prepare the onions and mushrooms (recipefollows).

8. Simmer the chicken cooking liquid in the casserole for a minute or two,skimming off the fat. Then raise the heat and boil rapidly, reducing the liquid to about 2 1/4 cups. Correct seasoning. Remove from heat and discard bay leaf.

9. Blend the butter and flour together into a smooth paste (buerremanie). Beatthe paste into the hot liquid with a wire whip. Bring to the simmer, stirring, and
simmer for a minute or two. The sauce should be thick enough to coat a spoonlightly.

10. Arrange the chicken in the casserole, place the mushrooms and onionsaround it and baste with the sauce. If this dish is not to be served immediately,
film the top of the sauce with stock or dot with small pieces of butter. Set asideuncovered. It can now wait indefinitely.

11. Shortly before serving, bring to the simmer, basting the chicken with thesauce. Cover and simmer slowly for 4 to 5 minutes, until the chicken is hotenough.

12. Sever from the casserole, or arrange on a hot platter. Decorate with spring
for parsley.

OignonsGlacés a Brun [Brown-braised Onions]

Ingredients

For 18 to 24 peeled white onions about 1 inch in diameter:
1 1/2 tablespoons butter
1 1/2 tablespoons oil
A 9-to 10-inch enameled skillet
1/2 cup of brown stock, canned beef bouillon, dry white
wine, red wine or water
Salt and pepper to taste
A medium herb bouquet: 3 parsley springs, 1/2 bay leaf, and
1/4 teaspoon thyme
tied in cheesecloth

Directions

When the butter and oil are bubbling the skillet, add the
onions and sauté over moderate heat for about 10 minutes,
rolling the onions
about so they will brown as evenly as possible. Be careful
not to break their
skins. You cannot expect to brown them uniformly.
Pour in the liquid, season to taste, and add the herb bouquet.
Cover and simmer
slowly for 40 to 50 minutes until the onions are perfectly
tender but retain their
shape, and the liquid has evaporated. Remove the herb
bouquet. Serve them as
they are.

Champignons Sautés Au Buerre [Sautéed Mushrooms]

Ingredients
A 10-inch enameled skillet
2 tablespoons butter
1 tablespoon oil
1/2 pound fresh mushrooms, washed, well dried, left whole if small, sliced or
quartered if large
1 to 2 tablespoons minced shallots or green onions (optional)
Salt and pepper

Directions
Place the skillet over high heat with the butter and oil. As soonas you see the butter foam has begun to subside, indicating that it is hot enough,
add the mushrooms. Toss and shake the pan for 4 to 5 minutes. During theirsauté the mushrooms will at first absorb the fat. In 2 to 3 minutes the fat will
reappear on their surface, and the mushrooms will begin to brown. As soon asthey have browned lightly, remove from heat.
Toss the shallots or green onions with the mushrooms. Sauté over moderate heatfor 2 minutes.
Sautéed mushrooms may be cooked in advance, set aside, then reheated whenneeded. Season to taste just before serving.

Flammekueche

Ingredients

The dough:
2 ½ teaspoons, or 1 package, dry yeast
2 ¼ to 2 ½ cups unbleached flour
1 cup lukewarm water
1 teaspoon salt
The topping:
1 cup cottage cheese or ricotta
1 cup cremefraiche or sour cream
2 medium onions, sliced into thin rounds
Salt and freshly ground black pepper to taste
12 ounces slab bacon, rind removed, cut into matchstick-size pieces

Preparation

1. Combine the water, yeast and one cup of the flour in a large mixingbowl. Stir until thoroughly blended and set aside to proof the yeast,about five minutes.

2. Once proofed, add the salt, then begin adding the remaining flour,little by little, until the dough is too stiff to stir. Place the dough on alightly floured work surface and begin kneading, adding additional flour if the dough is too sticky. Knead until the dough is smooth andsatiny, about 10 minutes.

3. Once kneaded, place the dough in a bowl, cover, and let rise at roomtemperature until double in bulk, about one hour.

4. Punch down and let rise again, covered, until double in bulk, aboutone hour.

5. Preheat the oven to 450 degrees.

6. Combine the onions, cheese, cremefraiche, salt and pepper and let sitfor 15 minutes to soften the onions.

7. Roll the dough on a lightly floured surface into a rectangle to fit alarge baking sheet, measuring about 12 1/2 by 15 inches. Place thedough on the baking sheet.

8. Spread the onion mixture over the dough right to the edge. Sprinklethe bacon evenly over the top, then sprinkle generously with pepper.

9. Bake just until the dough is crisp, 15 to 20 minutes. Serve immediately.

Raclette

Ingredients

1 lb. medium red-skinned new potatoes
1" x 1/2" batons
4 oz. slab bacon, cut into
1/4 tsp. cayenne
Freshly ground black pepper
1/2 bunch chives, chopped
1/2 lb. raclette, thinly sliced into square pieces
Salt

Preparation

1. Put potatoes into a medium pot, cover with cold water, and add 2 generouspinches salt. Bring to a boil over high heat, reduce heat to medium, and cookuntil potatoes are just soft when pierced with the tip of a knife, 10–15 minutes. Drain and set aside until cool enough to handle. Cut potatoes crosswise into1/2"-thick slices and set aside.

2. Meanwhile, put bacon into a small skillet and cook over medium heat, stirringoften, until crisp, about 10 minutes. Transfer bacon with a slotted spoon to paper towels to drain and set aside.

3. Preheat broiler. Divide potatoes between 4 medium ovenproof plates,arranging them to overlap slightly. Season each to taste with pepper and a pinchof the cayenne, sprinkle with some of the bacon, then cover with some of the

cheese. Put plates under broiler until cheese melts and bubbles and browns inplaces, 5-10 minutes. Garnish with chives.

ChoucrouteGarnie

Ingredients

2 tablespoons light brown sugar
1/3 cup kosher salt, plus more for seasoning 6 pounds
sauerkraut (in plastic
bags), drained 3 pounds pork back ribs or baby back ribs,
cut into 3 sections 1
large onion, coarsely chopped
1/4 cup duck or goose fat or peanut oil 20 juniper berries
4 large garlic cloves, coarsely chopped 1/2 teaspoon
caraway seeds
3 large bay leaves
3 cups chicken stock
1 teaspoon freshly ground black pepper 2 pounds Polish
kielbasa, skinned and
cut into 2-inch pieces 1 1/2 cups Riesling or Pinot Gris One
2-pound piece of
boneless boiled ham (3 to 4 inches wide), sliced 1/4 inch
thick 10 skinless hot
dogs
Assorted mustards, for serving
2 pounds medium potatoes (about 10), peeled

Directions

1. In a large, sturdy, resealable plastic bag, combine the 1/3 cup of kosher salt with the sugar. Add the pork ribs; shake well to thoroughly coat the ribs with the seasonings. Seal the bag and refrigerate

the ribs overnight or for up to 24 hours.

2. The next day, preheat the oven to 300°. Rinse thesauerkraut in cold water and squeeze dry. Set alarge roasting pan over 2 burners on high heat and melt the duck fat. Add the onion and garlic andcook over moderately low heat, stirring, untilsoftened, about 7 minutes. Stir in the sauerkraut,juniper berries, bay leaves, caraway seeds, blackpepper, stock and wine and bring to a rolling boilover high heat.

3. Meanwhile, rinse the pork ribs under cold water and pat dry. Nestle the pork ribs in the sauerkraut and bring back to a boil over moderately high heat. Cover tightly with foil and bake for 1 1/2 hours.

4. Remove the pork ribs from the sauerkraut. Cut down in between the ribs. Return the ribs to the sauerkraut and nestle in the kielbasa, hot dogs andham. Cover and bake until the meats are hot, about25 minutes. Discard the bay leaves.

5. Meanwhile, in a large saucepan, cover the potatoes with cold water, add salt and bring to a boil overhigh heat; cook the potatoes until tender whenpierced. Drain the potatoes and cover to keepwarm.

6. To serve, mound the hot sauerkraut in the center of very hot dinner plates and partially tuck in thepork ribs and the kielbasa. Arrange the hot dogsand ham around the sauerkraut. Alternatively, pilethe sauerkraut on a large heated platter and garnishwith the meats. Serve the choucroute with theboiled potatoes and assorted mustards.

Baeckeoffe

Ingredients

500 gm beef blade, cut into 5cm pieces 550 gm deboned lamb leg, cut into 5cm
pieces 550 gm pork loin, cut into 5cm pieces
4 (about 500gm) leeks, white parts only, cut into 5cm rounds
2 large (600gm)
Spanish onions, each cut into 8 wedges 4 cloves garlic, finely chopped
1 bouquet garni (see note)
750 ml Alsatian pinot blanc (see note) 75 gm butter
1 kg desiree potatoes, peeled and thinly sliced To serve: mixed green leaf salad

Method

1. Combine meats, leek, onion, garlic and bouquet garni in a large bowl. Season with freshly groundblackpepper, add wine, cover and marinateovernight in the refrigerator.

2. Preheat oven to 160C. Remove meat, vegetables and bouquet garni from the marinade,placing meat and vegetables each in separatebowls, reserving the marinade and bouquet garni.Heat 60gm butter in a large frying pan overmedium heat, add meat and cook for 5 minutes oruntil browned all over. Transfer to a bowl.

3. Grease a 4 litre-capacity (30cm long x 23cmwide) cast-iron or ovenproof casserole dish withremaining butter. Layer one-quarter of potatoes inbase and season to taste with sea

salt and freshlyground black pepper. Add one-third of meatmixture, then one-third of vegetables and reservedbouquet garni, seasoning to taste. Repeat twicewith remaining potatoes, meat and vegetables,seasoning to taste between layers, finishing with alayer of potatoes. Pour over reserved marinade,seal with foil, cover with lid and bake for 2½hours or until meat and vegetables are tender.
Serve immediately with salad on the side.

Quiche Lorraine

Ingredients

All-purpose flour, for dusting
Tart Dough
10 ounces slab bacon, cut into 3/4-by-1/4-by-1/4-inch strips
3 large eggs
2 cups heavy cream
3/4 teaspoon coarse salt
1/4 teaspoon freshly ground pepper

Directions

1. On a lightly floured work surface, roll out dough to 1/4 inch thick.Cut out a 13-inch circle from dough. Press dough onto bottom and upsides of an 11-inch tart pan with aremovable bottom; trim doughflush with top edge of pan. Prick bottom all over with a fork. Transferto a rimmedbaking sheet. Freeze until firm, about 30 minutes. Preheat oven to 400 degrees.

2. Line tart shell with parchment paper, and fill with pie weights or driedbeans. Bake until dough starts to feel firm on the edges, about 20minutes. Remove parchment and weights; continue baking until crustis pale golden brown, about 10 minutes. Let cool completely on awire rack. Leave oven on.

3. Cook bacon in a large skillet over medium heat until browned, about10 minutes. Transfer with a slotted spoon to paper towels to drain.

4. Whisk eggs, cream, salt, and pepper in a medium bowl. Pour mixtureinto tart shell, and scatter the bacon strips ontop. Bake until puffedand pale golden brown, about 30 minutes. Let cool at least 30 minutesbefore serving.

Soup

Soupe à L'oignon

Ingredients

9 tablespoons butter, softened
1 baguette, cut into 1/2-inch slices (about 25 to 30)
8 medium yellow onions, thinly sliced (about 12 cups)
9 ounces Emmental cheese, finely grated
1 cup tomato purée.
1 tablespoon kosher salt, more to taste

Preparation

1. Toast the baguette slices and let them cool. Spread a generous layer of butter
on each slice (you will need about 5 tablespoons), then lay the slices closetogether on a baking sheet and top with all but 1/2 cup of cheese.

2. In a large saucepan, melt the remaining 4 tablespoons butter over mediumheat. Add the onions, season with salt and sauté, stirring occasionally, until verysoft and golden, about 15 minutes.

3. In a 5-quart casserole, arrange a layer of bread slices (about 1/3 of them).Spread 1/3 of the onions on top, followed by 1/3 of the tomato purée. Repeat for two more layers. Sprinkle with the remaining 1/2 cup cheese. To avoid boilingover, the casserole must not be more than 2/3 full.

4. In a saucepan, bring 1 1/2 quarts water to a boil. Add the salt. Very slowlypour the salted water into the casserole, near the edge, so that the liquid rises justto the top layer of cheese without covering it. (Depending on the size of yourcasserole, you may need more or less water.) 5. Preheat the oven to 350 degrees.Put the casserole on the stove and simmer uncovered for 30 minutes, thentransfer to the oven and bake uncovered for 1 hour. The soup is ready when the surface looks like a crusty, golden cake and the inside is unctuous and so wellblended that it is impossible to discern either cheese or onion. Each person isserved some of the baked crust and some of the inside, which should be thick butnot completely without liquid.

Soupe de Poisson

Ingredients

1 large onion
¼ c olive oil
1 small fennel bulb, sliced 2 leeks, chopped
3-4 lbs fish (I used whole porgie, sardines, whole dorado,
blue fish, Spanishmackerel, striped bass and a carcass)
Wright recommended using ¼ oily fish andthe rest whiter
fish (not salmon).
Make sure you get some whole fish or haveyour fishmonger
give you some carcasses for the soup. To make a rich broth,
you need bones and heads!
2 ½ quarts water
1 T tomato paste
1 pound tomatoes, chopped (or 1 can) bouquet garni
(parsley, thyme and bay)
3garlic cloves
½ t cayenne
pinch saffron (from Marx Foods) 1 oz Absinthe or Pernod or
1 T cognac (Iadded more after cooking and straining) 4
drops Aftelierpetitgrain or 1 10" strip
orange peel and 1 t orange flower water (do this to taste... I
added more aftercooking and straining) rouille (see recipe
below) 3 oz vermicelli, cooked
(optional) ½ lb gruyere, grated

Directions

Heat the olive oil and cook the onion leeks and fennel about 6 minutes overmedium high heat. Add the water, fish, tomatoes, tomato paste, garlic, bouquetgarni, saffron and cayenne, season with salt and black pepper and stir. Let boilfor 45 minutes. Add orange zest and Absinthe/brandy and boil 8 more minutes.The fish will have disintegrated at this point.Take out the bones and skin and orange peel. Pass the rest through a food milland toss everything that doesn't go through after several turns. If you don't havea food mill, press through a strainer to get some of the solids into the broth. Addthe vermicelli if you wish. Top with croutons with the rouille and the gratedcheese.

Rouille

Ingredients

½ c fish broth

1 ½ c French bread (crust removed) 1 t salt

4-5 peeled garlic cloves pinch saffron (from Marx Foods) ½ t ground red chili

pepper (Wright recommended chili de arbol and I used Marx foods) pepper

1 large egg yolk

5 T butter

1 ¼ c olive oil (save ¼ c for toasts) 40 slices bread

Directions

1. Soak the diced bread in the fish broth. Squeeze the broth out. Mash the garliccloves in a mortar with the salt until mushy. Place the bread, mashed garlic(saving 1 garlic clove for the croutes), red pepper, saffron, egg yolk and blackpepper in a food processor and blend for 30 seconds then pour in 1 cup olive oilthrough the feed tube in a slow, thin, steady stream while the machine isrunning. Refrigerate for 1 hour before serving. Store whatever you don't use in the refrigerator for up to a week.

2. Meanwhile, prepare the croutes. In a large skillet, melt the butter with theremaining 1/4 cup olive oil over medium heat with the remaining crushed garlicuntil it begins to turn light brown. Remove and discard the garlic.

3. Lightly brush both sides of each bread slice with the melted butter and oil andset aside. When all the slices are

brushed place them back in the skillet and cookuntil they are a very light brown on both sides. Set aside until needed.

Soupe au Pistou

Ingredients

1/4 cup / 60 ml olive oil

1 pound / 16 oz / 450 g dried flageolet beans, soaked for at least 4 hours,

preferably overnight, then drained 2 medium leeks, trimmed and chopped 4

medium onions, chopped

12 cups / 3 liters water

4 stalks celery, chopped

4 medium yellow potatoes, chopped

1 28-ounce can, whole tomatoes, well drained, chopped 1/4 pound / 4 oz.

stellette (tiny star) pasta, or other small pasta 1 bouillon cube, optional

1/2 cup (a big handful) chard stems, finely chopped 3 small zucchini, chopped

2 teaspoons salt, or to taste

Pistou

scant 3/4 teaspoon fine grain sea salt

1 tablespoon crushed garlic

1 tomato (from above), well chopped

4 1/2 cups 2 oz 60 g basil leaves, torn into small pieces

1 cup 2 oz 60 g grated aged Gruyere cheese

1/4 cup / 60 ml extra-virgin olive oil

Directions

In your largest soup pot heat the oil, then add the onions, leeks, and celery. Sautefor about 5 minutes, then stir in the soaked beans and 12 cups water. Bring to aboil, dial back to a simmer, then cook for about 15 minutes. Reserve one of thetomatoes for the pistou, then stir the remaining tomatoes into the pot, then thepotatoes. Cook for another 15-20 minutes, or until the beans seem like they arenearly cooked. Add a bouillon cube if you like, then the pasta, and simmer for 5minutes. Add the zucchini and the chard stems and cook for another 3 minutes.Stir in salt - perhaps less if you used a salty bouillon - essentially, you want tosalt to taste. At this point the pasta should be cooked through, as well as all thebeans and vegetables. For the soup to taste good, you really need to get the rightamount of salt in it - just bemindful of this, and adjust if needed.

While the soup is cooking, you can make the pistou. I use a mortar and pestle,but you can use a food processor if you like. Pound the garlic with the salt into apaste. Add the basil a handful at a time and pound and grind until nearly smooth. Add the tomatoes, then gradually stir in the olive oil a bit at a time. Stir in thecheese, then chill until ready to use.Ladle soup into bowls and top with a generous dollop ofpistou.

Desserts

Bûche de Noël

Ingredients

FOR THE ICING:

12 oz. semisweet chocolate

2/3 cup heavy cream 8 tbsp. unsalted butter

FOR THE MERINGUE:

10 tbsp. sugar

2 pinches cream of tartar

2 large egg whites

1/2 tsp. vanilla extract

1/4 cup cocoa powder

1/2 cup confectioners' sugar Pinch salt

FOR THE ROULADE:

2 tbsp. softened butter

7 egg whites

2 tbsp. sugar 8 oz. bittersweet chocolate, finely chopped

1 cup heavy cream

2 tbsp. dark rum

FOR THE FILLING:

4 oz. semisweet chocolate

6 tbsp. sugar

3 egg yolks

12 tbsp. unsalted butter

Method

1. For the icing: Melt chocolate and butter in the top of a double boiler set oversimmering water over medium-low heat, whisking often. Remove from heat andgradually whisk in cream. Transfer to a medium bowl and set aside at room temperature, stirring occasionally, until icing thickens, about 4 hours. (Don'trefrigerate; it makes icing hard to spread.) 2. For the meringue: Preheat oven to200°. Combine sugar and 1/4 cup water in a small saucepan, cover, and bring toa boil over medium-high heat, swirling pan several times until sugar hasdissolved, 1–2 minutes. Uncover pan and continue to boil until syrup reachessoftball stage or 236° on a candy thermometer, about 4 minutes more. Put eggwhites in the bowl of a standing mixer fitted with a whisk and beat on mediumspeed until frothy, then add cream of tartar and salt. Gradually increase speed tohigh and beat until soft peaks form, about 30 seconds. Slowly pour in sugarsyrup while continuing to beat until whites cool to room temperature and become thick and shiny, about 10 minutes. Stir in vanilla. Use a rubber spatulato transfer meringue to a pastry bag fitted with a 1/4" plain pastry tip. To makemeringue mushrooms, hold pastry tip perpendicular to a parchment paper-linedbaking sheet and pipe meringue into the shapes of mushroom caps and stems ofvarious sizes, then set aside for 5 minutes. Lightly moisten a fingertip in coldwater and smooth out any "tails" left behind on mushroom caps. Bake meringuesfor 1 1/2 hours. Turn off oven and allow meringues to rest in oven until dry andcrisp, about 1 hour. Bore a small, shallow hole in center of underside of each

mushroom cap with the tip of a paring knife. "Glue" stems to caps by dippingtips of stems into icing, then sticking into holes in caps. Sift a little cocoapowder on tops of caps. Meringues can be stored in an airtight container at roomtemperature for several days.

3. For the roulade: Preheat oven to 375°. Line a 16 1/2" × 12" heavy baking panwith buttered parchment paper, cut large enough to hang over sides of the pan byabout 1". Put chocolate in a large mixing bowl and set aside. Bring cream just toa boil in a saucepan over medium heat, then pour over chocolate and whisk untilsmooth. Set aside to cool. Beat egg whites in the bowl of a standing mixer fittedwith a whisk on medium speed until frothy; increase speed to medium-high andgradually add sugar, beating constantly, then increase speed to high and beatuntil stiff, glossy peaks form, 30-40 seconds more. (Don't overbeat.) Mix one-third of the whites into chocolate using a rubber spatula, then gently fold inremaining whites in two batches, taking care not to deflate batter. Spread inprepared pan and bake until a toothpick inserted in center comes out clean, 10–12 minutes. Set aside to cool in the pan.

4. For the filling: Melt chocolate with 2 tbsp. water in the top of a double boilerset over simmering water over medium heat. Stir to combine, then set aside to cool. Combine sugar and 3 tbsp. water in a small heavy saucepan; cover andbring to a boil over medium heat, swirling pan several times until sugar has dissolved, about 1 minute. Uncover and continue to boil until syrup reaches thesoftball stage or 236° on a candy

thermometer, about 5 minutes more.Meanwhile, beat yolks in the bowl of a standing mixer fitted with a whisk onhigh speed until thick and pale yellow, about 3 minutes. Reduce speed tomedium and gradually pour in hot syrup. Beat constantly until mixture cools toroom temperature, about 10 minutes. Allow butter to soften, then beat into eggmixture 1 tbsp. at a time, waiting until it's completely incorporated before addingmore; continue beating until thick and smooth, about 5 minutes total. Stir incooled chocolate and set aside.

5. To assemble the bûche: Transfer roulade with parchment to a clean worksurface, sprinkle with rum, then spread filling evenly over top using a metal spatula. Grab the long edge of the parchment paper with two hands and gentlyroll roulade onto itself, pulling off paper as you roll. To make stumps, diagonally cut a 2" length from each end of bûche; then, to make the stumps thinner thanthe bûche, partially unroll each piece, trim off flap, and discard. Set stumps aside.

6. Using two long metal spatulas, carefully transfer bûche to a serving platterlined with strips of waxed paper. "Glue" stumps onto bûche with some of the icing. Melt 1/4 cup of icing in a saucepan over low heat, then spoon it overstumps to coat completely. Spread remaining icing on bûche, dragging spatula along icing to simulate tree bark. Remove waxed-paper strips. Decorate withmushrooms, then sift confectioners' sugar over mushrooms and bûche.

Tartetatin

Ingredients

All-purpose flour, for dusting
4 tablespoons unsalted butter, cut into small pieces, plus
more for pan
1 cup sugar
1/2 Pate Brisee, chilled
2 to 3 medium baking apples, such as Cortland or Rome
(about 1 1/4
pounds), peeled, cored, and cut into quarters
Dash of lemon juice
Cremefraiche, for serving (optional)

Directions

1. Preheat oven to 425 degrees. Generously butter a 9-inch metal pieplate; set aside. Line a baking sheet with parchment paper, and setaside. On a lightly floured work surface, roll out the dough to a 9-inchround, about 1/4-inch thick. Place dough on the prepared bakingsheet, and chill until firm, about 30 minutes.

2. Meanwhile, in a small saucepan, mix together the sugar, 2 tablespoons cold water, and the lemon juice to form a thick syrup.Bring to a boil over high heat, swirling pan; cook until the mixtureturns medium amber, about 3 minutes. Remove the pan from heat,and pour the mixture onto the bottom of the prepared pie plate.Immediately add the butter, distributing evenly.

3. Arrange the apples, rounded sides down, around the bottom of the panin a circular pattern, starting from the outside and working in, fittingthem as close together as possible (the apples will be the top of thetart when served). Drape the chilled dough round over the apples tocover the mixture completely.

4. Bake until golden, about 25 minutes. Meanwhile, line a rimmedbaking sheet with a clean non-stick baking mat. Remove the tart fromthe oven, and immediately invert onto the mat, working quickly butcarefully to avoid contact with the hot caramel. Using tongs, carefullylift the pie plate off of the tart. Transfer the sheet to a wire rack tocool. Serve warm with crème-fraiche, if using.

Cherry Clafoutis

Ingredients
1 ¼ cups milk
1 tbsp. unsalted butter, softened
2 tbsp. kirsch
6 tbsp. sugar
6 eggs
1 tbsp. vanilla extract
¾ cup flour
Kosher salt, to taste
Confectioners' sugar, for dusting
3 cups black cherries, pitted or unpitted

Instructions
1. Heat oven to 425°. Grease a 9″ cast-iron skillet or baking dish with butter; setaside. Combine milk, sugar, kirsch, vanilla, eggs, and salt in a blender. Blend for a few seconds to mix Ingredients, then add flour and blend until smooth, about 1minute.
2. Pour batter into buttered skillet, then distribute cherries evenly over top. Bakeuntil a skewer inserted into batter comes out clean and a golden brown crust hasformed on top and bottom of clafoutis, about 30 minutes. Dust withconfectioners' sugar before serving.

Roasted Rhubarb Clafouti

Ingredients
For the Rhubarb:

2 tablespoons granulated sugar
2 cups (8 1/2 ounces, about 3 long stalks) diced rhubarb
1/2 teaspoon cinnamon
For the Clafouti
1/3 cup (2 1/2 ounces) granulated sugar
3 large eggs
1 teaspoon vanilla extract
1/2 cup (2 1/2 ounces) all-purpose flour
1 cup (8 ounces) whole milk
1 teaspoon lemon zest
pinch of salt

Instructions

Heat the oven to 350°F.

Combine the rhubarb with the sugar and cinnamon in a small bowl and set asidefor 5-10 minutes to dissolve the sugars and begin extracting the rhubarb juices.

Spread the rhubarb in the bottom of an 8x8" baking dish or 9" pie pan. Roastuncovered for 15-20 minutes, until the rhubarb is soft and the juices arebubbling. Allow to cool until the rhubarb is just warm to the touch.Whisk together the eggs, sugar, and vanilla. Whisk in the milk. Whisk in the flour, lemon zest, and salt. (To avoid clumps, sift the flour into the bowl througha strainer.) This batter can be prepared up to 30 minutes ahead of time.Pour the batter over the roasted rhubarb and bake for 35-40 minutes (still at350°F).

When it's done, the clafouti should be puffed around the edges and atoothpick inserted in the middle should come out clean. It's ok if the middle stilljiggles slightly, and the edges will collapse once the clafouti starts to cool.The longer it cools, the most set the clafouti becomes. For a loose pudding-likedessert, serve while still warm from the oven. For a firmer custard, allow to coolto room temperature or serve chilled. If you're feeling fancy, sift a littleconfectioner's sugar over the top just before serving.

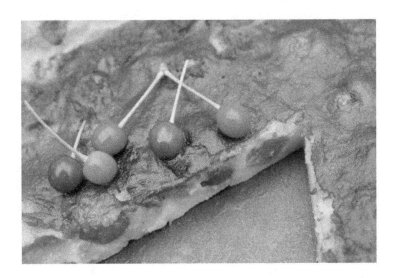

Crêpes Suzette

Ingredients

For Crêpes
3/4 cup all-purpose flour
2 large eggs
1/8 teaspoon salt
1/2 cup milk
1/3 cup cold water
1/2 teaspoon sugar
1 tablespoon melted unsalted butter, plus more butter for the skillet
1 tablespoon canola oil
For Orange Butter
1/4 cup plus 2 tablespoons sugar, plus more for sprinkling
6 tablespoons unsalted butter, softened, plus more for buttering
1/4 cup Grand Marnier
2 tablespoons Cognac
1/3 cup fresh orange juice
1 tablespoon finely grated orange zest

Instructions

1. In a medium bowl, whisk together the eggs, flour, milk, salt and sugaruntil smooth; the batter will be thick. Whisk in the water, oil andmelted butter.
2. Heat a 6-inch crêpe pan or nonstick skillet and rub with a little butter.

Add 2 tablespoons of the batter and tilt the skillet to distribute thebatter evenly, pouring any excess batter back into the bowl. Cookover moderately high heat until the edges of the crêpe curl up andstart to brown, 45 seconds. Flip the crêpe and cook for 10 secondslonger, until a few brown spots appear on the bottom. Tap the crêpeout onto a baking sheet . Repeat with the remaining batter to make 12 crêpes, buttering the skillet a few times as necessary.

3. In a mini food processor, blend the 6 tablespoons of butter with ¼ cup of the sugar and the orange zest. With themachine on, graduallyadd the orange juice until incorporated.

4. Preheat the broiler. Butter a large rimmed baking sheet and sprinklelightly with sugar. Place 2 rounded teaspoons of the orange butter inthe center of each crêpe. Fold the crêpes in half and in half again toform triangles; arrange on the prepared baking sheet, pointing them inthe same direction and overlapping slightly. Sprinkle with theremaining 2 tablespoons of sugar and broil on the middle shelf of theoven until they begin to caramelize, about 2 minutes. Using a longspatula, transfer the crêpes to a heatproof platter.

5. Meanwhile, in a small saucepan, heat the Grand Marnier and cognac.Ignite carefully with a long-handled match and pour the flamingmixture over the crêpes. Tilt the platter and, with a spoon, carefullybaste the crêpes until the flames subside. Serve right away.

Paris-Brest

Ingredients
For the Pastry Wreath
1 stick (1/2 cup) unsalted butter, cut into pieces
1 cup all purpose flour
1 teaspoon sugar (optional)
1/2 teaspoon salt
4 large eggs, plus 1 large egg for egg wash
For Filling and Decorating
1 1/2 cup heavy cream
1/2 teaspoon pure vanilla extract
3 tablespoons confectioners' sugar, plus more for dusting
Pastry Cream

Directions
1. Male the pastry wreath: Preheat oven to 425 degrees. Trace a 9-inchcircle onto a sheet of parchment. Flip parchment, making sure pencilmark is still visible, and place on a baking sheet.
2. In a medium saucepan over medium-high heat, combine butter, sugar,salt, and 1 cup water. Bring to a boil and immediately remove fromheat. Using a wooden spoon, quickly stir in the flour until combined.
3. Return pan to medium-high heat and cook, stirring vigorously, untilmixture pulls away from the sides and a film forms on the bottom ofthe pan, about 3 minutes.
4. Remove from heat and transfer contents to a bowl to cool slightly,about 3 minutes. Add eggs, one at a time, stirring

vigorously aftereach addition, and waiting until each is entirely incorporated beforeadding the next egg. Use immediately.

5. Transfer pate a choux dough to a pastry bag fitted with a 1/2-inchplain round tip. Pipe a tiny dot under each corner of parchment,pressing to adhere parchment to baking sheet. Then pipe dough,tracing outline, into sixteen 1 3/4-inch mounds, holding pastry bagupright and keeping pressure consistent.

6. Whisk remaining egg with pinch salt. Brush egg over top of pastrywreath.

7. Bake until pastry just starts to puff, about 10 minutes. Reduce oventemperature to 375 degrees. Bake until pastry is fully puffed andgolden brown, about 30 minutes.

8. Turn oven off, remove wreath, and pierce top and sides about 8 timesusing the tip of a sharp knife to release steam. Return to oven, andprop door open with a wooden spoon. Let stand for 1 hour to dry.

9. Transfer pastry wreath on parchment to a wire rack. Let coolcompletely.

10. Fill and decorate the pastry wreath: Whisk heavy cream, confectioners' sugar, and vanilla until soft peaks form. Separate pastrywreath into top and bottom halves using a serrated knife.

11. Spread about 1 1/2 cups pastry cream over bottom ring. Pipe whipped cream in a swirl using 1/2-inch closed star tip. Reposition top piecesof pastry wreath over filling. Dust with confectioners' sugar.

Mini gâteau Paris-Brest

Ingredients
For the choux pastry
50g butter
70g plain flour
2 large eggs
For the filling
250ml double cream
1 tsp vanilla paste or extract
2 tbsp toasted flaked almonds, chopped
150g white chocolate
140g crystallised fruits, chopped
icing sugar, for dusting

Method

1. Heat the oven to 200C/180C fan/gas 6. Line a large baking sheet withbaking paper and mark 8 circles about 8-9cm across using a glass ormug. Turn the paper over. Sift the flour onto a sheet of baking paper.
Put the butter and 150ml water into a pan, then bring slowly to theboil until the butter has melted. When the water is bubbling, removequickly from the heat, tip in the flour all at once and beat quickly witha wooden spoon until it forms a dough that leaves the side of the panclean. Remove from the heat and cool for 3 mins.

2. Lightly beat the eggs with a fork. Add the egg to the dough gradually,beating well with each addition until the dough is smooth and glossy.

Put this dough into a piping bag fitted with a large plain nozzle (about2cm across) or use a large food bag with the corner snipped off. Pipe8 thick rings onto the baking sheet using the marked circles as aguide.

3. Bake the buns for 20-25 mins until crisp and golden, then split themcarefully in half through the centre using a sharp knife in a sawingaction; return to the oven for 5 mins. Transfer to a cooling rack,taking care to keep the tops and bottoms together, and leave to cool.Whip the cream to soft peaks and stir in the vanilla. Melt 100g of thechocolate for 1-2 mins in a microwave. Leave to cool slightly, thenfold into the cream.

4. Stir half the crystallised fruit and the almonds through the cream. Fillthe choux rings with the mixture using two teaspoons. Melt theremaining chocolate and drizzle over the choux rings. Scatter withcrystallised fruit and leave to set. Dust with icing sugar beforeserving.

Chocolate éclairs

Ingredients
For the choux pastry
4 tbsp water
4 tbsp whole milk
50g/2oz unsalted butter, at room temperature
100g/4oz plain flour
1 tsp caster sugar
pinch sea salt
4 medium free-range eggs, beaten
For the filling
450g/1lb pastry cream (crème patissière), at room temperature (see Top recipe tip below)
20g/¾oz unsweetened chocolate, 100% cocoa solids
1 tbsp strong cocoa powder, sifted
For the glaze
1 tbsp cocoa powder
200g/7oz white fondant icing
1-2 tsp water

Preparation
1. Preheat the oven to 170C/325F/Gas 3.
2. For the choux pastry, place the water, milk, butter, sugar and salt in amedium saucepan over a high heat and bring the mixture to a boil.

3. Remove the pan from the heat and, using a wooden spoon, quicklybeat in the flour until the mixture is completely smooth.

4. Turn the heat down to medium, return the pan to the hob and cook forabout one minute, beating all the time, or until the mixture comesaway from the edge of the pan.

5. Remove the pan from the heat and gradually beat in the eggs until youhave a smooth, dropping consistency. You are looking for themixture to just drop from the spoon, not run off it; you may not needall of the egg to reach this stage.

6. Transfer the paste to a large piping bag fitted with a 1.5cm/½in flutednozzle and let the mixture to cool for about five minutes in the bag tostiffen slightly before you begin the piping.

7. Line a large baking tray with greaseproof paper and pipe on 12éclairs, each about 15cm/6in long. Alternatively, for a moreprofessional and uniform finish, pipe four rows of pastry, each about36cm/14in long, onto a non-stick tray and freeze. Cut the frozen stripsinto three and either defrost and cook as below, or bake from frozenand add five minutes to the cooking time.

8. Bake the éclairs in the preheated oven for 30-35 minutes or untilgolden-brown, then transfer to a rack and leave to cool.

9. For the filling, melt the chocolate in a bowl over a pan of simmeringwater. Do not let the bottom of the bowl touch the water or thechocolate will burn.

10. Pour the melted chocolate into the pastry cream, mix in the cocoapowder and whisk together to a smooth

consistency. You could chillthe mixture at this point for 30 minutes, then whisk again before youfill the éclairs, to give a creamier mouth-feel to the filling.

11. When you are ready to fill the éclairs, transfer the filling to a pipingbag fitted with a 0.5cm/¼in nozzle. Pierce the underside of each éclairfour times with the tip of the nozzle, gently squirting a little of thefilling into the éclair as you do so.

12. For the glaze, gently warm the fondant in a small pan over a low heatuntil it reaches body temperature.

13. Stir in the cocoa powder and enough of the water to make a smoothpaste, then transfer to a piping bag fitted with a 1.5cm/½in nozzle.

14. Pipe the glaze onto the top of each éclair, removing any excess withthe back of your finger, then place in the fridgefor the glaze to setbefore serving.

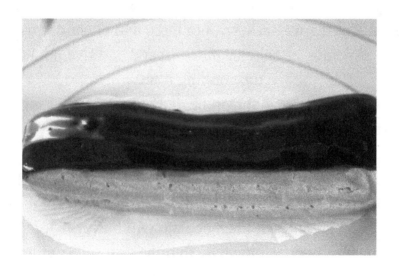

KouignAmann

tablespoon (12 g) active dry yeast, not instant ¾ cup (175 ml) tepid water
1 cup (200 g) sugar (which will be divided later) (Plus additional sugar for
rolling out the pastry) 2 cups (260 g) all-purpose flour
½ teaspoon sea salt
1 stick salted butter (110 g), cut into ½-inch (2 cm) cubes and chilled 2-3
tablespoons additional salted butter, melted

Preparation

1. In a medium bowl, dissolve the yeast in the water with a pinch of sugar. Stirbriefly, then let stand for 10 minutes until foamy.
2. Gradually stir the flour and salt. The dough should be soft, but not too sticky.Lightly dust your countertop with flour and transfer the dough onto it.Knead the dough with your hands until the dough is smooth and elastic, about 3 minutes. If the dough is very sticky, knead in just enough flour, one tablespoonat a time, until the dough doesn't stick to your hands.
3. Brush a medium bowl with melted butter, put the dough ball into the bowl.Cover, and let rest in a warm place for 1 hour.
4. Meanwhile, line a dinner plate with plastic wrap and set aside.

5. On a lightly floured countertop, roll the dough into a rectangle about 12″ x18″ with the shorter sides to your left and right.

The dough may be sticky and difficult to handle. Use a metal pastry scraper tocoax the dough into shape, and a minimal sprinkling of flour, as necessary.Distribute the cubed butter in the center of the dough and sprinkle with ¼ cup (50 gr) of sugar. Grab the left side of the dough, lift and fold it over the center,than do the same with the right side (like a letter). You should have whatresembles a 3-level pastry.

6. Sprinkle the entire length of the dough with ¼ cup (50 gr) of sugar and(without rolling) fold again into thirds, asbefore. Place on the plastic wrap-covered dinner plate and chill for 1 hour.

(At this point, wipe excess flour from the countertop and dust the countertopwith a rather liberal handful of sugar for rolling out the pastry again.)

7. Oncechilled, remove dough from refrigerator.Ease it away from the plastic onto the sugar-covered countertop.

(Use more sugar than shown. I was busy doing double-duty as the photographerand baker.) Top the dough with ¼ cup (50 gr) of sugar, press it in a bit with yourhands, and roll into a rectangle for the last time.Again, fold into thirds and let rest in the refrigerator for 30-60 minutes.

8. Preheat oven to 425° F (220° C) and brush a 9-inch (23cm) pie plate,preferably non-stick, with melted butter.

9. Remove dough from refrigerator. Roll dough into a circle about the size of thebaking pan. It will be sticky; dusting the

top with a sprinkle of sugar will help.Once rolled, lift the
dough and coax it into the pan. (It will want to break. If so,
fold it in half and quickly slide something flat under it, like
the metal benchscrape AND a metal spatula and quickly slip
it into the pan. If it does break, justpiece it back together in
the pan.) 10. Sprinkle with the remaining ¼ cup (50 gr)
of sugar and drizzle with 1 tablespoon melted butter.
Bake for 40-45 minutes, until the top is deeply caramelized.
Let stand a fewminutes, then run a spatula around the edges
to release the KouignAmann andslide the cake from the pan
onto a cooling rack.

CremeBrulee

Ingredients

1 vanilla bean, split and scraped 1 quart heavy cream
6 large egg yolks
1 cup vanilla sugar, divided
2 quarts hot water

Directions

Preheat the oven to 325 degrees F.

Place the cream, vanilla bean and its pulp into a medium saucepan set overmedium-high heat and bring to a boil.

Remove from the heat, cover and allow tosit for 15 minutes.

Remove the vanilla bean and reserve for another use.

In a medium bowl, whisk together 1/2 cup sugar and the egg yolks until wellblended and it just starts to lighten in color.

Add the cream a little at a time,stirring continually. Pour the liquid into 6 (7 to 8-ounce) ramekins. Place theramekins into a large cake pan or roasting pan. Pour enough hot water into thepan to come halfway up the sides of the ramekins. Bake just until the crème brulee is set, but still trembling in the center, approximately40 to 45 minutes.

Remove the ramekins from the roasting pan and refrigerate for at least 2 hoursand up to 3 days.

Remove the cremebrulee from the refrigerator for at least 30 minutes prior tobrowning the sugar on top. Divide the remaining 1/2 cup vanilla sugar equallyamong the 6 dishes and spread evenly on top. Using a torch, melt the sugar and form a crispy top. Allow the cremebrulee to sit for at least 5 minutes beforeserving.

Pithiviers

Ingredients

For the Frangipane
2/3 cup blanched whole almonds, toasted
1 egg
1 tablespoon dark rum
6 tablespoons butter, softened
1/2 cup sugar
2 tablespoons flour
1/2 teaspoon almond extract
For Assembling
All-purpose flour, for dusting
1 pound Puff Pastry, about 1/3 recipe
1 egg yolk
1 tablespoon heavy cream

Directions

1. Prepare the Puff Pastry.
2. Make the frangipane: In the bowl of a food processor, blend thealmonds and the sugar until very fine. Add the butter, egg, rum, flour,and almond extract and process until smooth. Wrap in plastic wrapand shape into a 6-inch round. Freeze until firm, at least 45 minutes.
3. On a lightly floured work surface, roll out puff pastry into a rectangleabout 18 by 9 inches and 1/8 inch thick. Using a 9-inch cake pan as aguide, cut two 9-inch rounds from the dough with a very sharp paringknife or pastry wheel. Using a 1-inch circular biscuit cutter or a largeround pastry tip, cut

out a steam vent from the center of the top round.Place rounds on a baking sheet and freeze until very firm but still pliable, about 20 minutes.

4. In a small bowl, whisk together the egg yolk and heavy cream for theegg wash.

5. Preheat the oven to 375 degrees. Remove dough from freezer. Placefrozen frangipane round in the center of the bottom dough circle.

Brush the border with egg wash, taking special care not to let the eggwash drip down the sides, which would inhibit proper puffing duringbaking. Place the second round on top, and press to seal, using yourfingers. Using a small paring knife, score the top of each Pithivier in acircular, decorative cross-hatch pattern. With a small paring knife, score around edges in 1/4-inch increments. Transfer Pithiviers to abaking sheet sprayed well with water and chill for at least 1 hour.

6. Remove Pithiviers from freezer. Brush top with egg wash, againbeing careful not to let any excess drip down over cut edge of dough.Bake until puffed and golden brown, about 45 to 50 minutes.

7. Transfer Pithiviers to a wire rack, and let cool at least 20 minutesbefore serving.

French Apple Cake

Ingredients
1 3/4 cups sugar
1/4 cup (1/2 stick) unsalted butter 3/4 teaspoon ground cinnamon 1/3 cup water
1 cup all purpose flour 2 large Granny Smith apples (about 1 1/4 pounds),
peeled, cored, thinly sliced 1/4 teaspoon salt
1 teaspoon baking powder 2 large eggs
3 large egg yolks
2 teaspoons vanilla
2 tablespoons Calvados, applejack or other brandy 1/2 cup (1 stick) unsalted
butter, melted

Preparation
Preheat oven to 350°F. Butter 9-inch-diameter cake pan with 2-inch-high sides.Coat pan with sugar; tap out excess. Melt 1/4 cup butter in heavy large skilletover medium-high heat. Stir in 3/4 cup sugar, water and cinnamon and bring to boil. Add apples and cook until apples are just tender, turning frequently, about15 minutes. Remove apples, using slotted spoon, and arrange decoratively in bottom of pan. Continue boiling liquid in skillet until thick and syrupy, about 4minutes. Pour over apples.
Sift flour, baking powder and salt into small bowl. Whisk remaining 1 cup sugar,egg yolks, eggs, Calvados and vanilla in large bowl to blend. Gently stir in dry

Ingredients. Fold in 1/2 cup melted butter. Pour batter over apples in pan. Bakeuntil toothpick inserted into center of cake comes out clean, about 45 minutes.Cool cake in pan 5 minutes. Run small sharp knife around side of pan to loosen cake. Turn cake out onto platter. Serve warm or at room temperature.

Far-breton

4 eggs
300 g pitted dried prunes
1 tsp salted butter
75 cl full-cream milk
225 g plain flour (sifted)
8 g vanilla sugar
125 g caster sugar
Dark rum (enough to cover the prunes in a small bowl)
A pinch of salt.

Preparation
Preheat oven 200 °C.
Place pitted dried prunes in a small bowl and pour enough rum to cover theprunes. Cover and set aside for 48 hours at room temperature. The prunes willsoak up most of the rum. Drain the soaked prunes and keep the remaining rum. Set aside. In a saucepanheat the milk until it simmers. Remove the thin layer of film that might haveformed. Beat the eggs until fluffy, then pour slowly to the sifted flour, whisking away. Add the warm milk slowly, sugar, vanilla sugar, a pinch of salt andcontinue whisking. Pour remaining rum into batter and set the prunes aside.
Line a rectangle or oval oven-proof dish (27 cm length/5.5 cm depth approx.)with butter and pour in half of the batter. Place prunes evenly all over the dishand continue pouring the remaining batter. Place in the oven for 35 minutes –

when the 'far' is slightly golden, take it out of the oven and spread salted butterall over. Lower the oven temperature to 180°C and bake for another 10 minutes.Let the far rest until cooled and serve (it can also be served warm to your liking).

Chef Marino

Gateau Basque

Ingredients

2 cups all-purpose flour
3/4 teaspoons baking powder
1 egg beaten with a splash of water, for the glaze 1 stick
plus 2 tablespoons (5
ounces) unsalted butter, at room temperature
1 large egg, at room temperature
1/4 cup (packed) light brown sugar
1/4 cup sugar 1/2 teaspoon pure vanilla extract
3/4 to 1 cup thick cherry jam or an equal amount of vanilla
pastry cream
1/2 teaspoon salt

Preparation

Whisk together the flour, baking powder and salt and keep at hand. Working in a mixer fitted with the paddle attachment or in a bowl with a handmixer, beat the butter and both sugars together on medium speed for about 3minutes, or until smooth. Add the egg and beat another 2 minutes or so, scrapingdown the sides of the bowl as needed. The mixture may look curdled, but that'sOK. Add vanilla and mix for about a minute more. Then reduce the mixer speedto low and add the dry Ingredients in two or three additions, mixing only untilthey're fully incorporated into the dough.

Place a large sheet of plastic wrap or wax paper on your work surface and puthalf of the very soft and sticky dough in

138

the center of the sheet. Cover withanother piece of plastic or wax paper, then roll the dough into a circle just a little larger than 8 inches in diameter. As you're rolling, turn the dough over and liftthe plastic or paper frequently, so that you don't roll it into the dough and form creases. Repeat with the other half of the dough.

Put the dough on a cutting board or baking sheet and refrigerate it for about 3hours or for up to 3 days.

When you're ready to assemble and bake the gateau, center a rack in the ovenand preheat the oven to 350. Generously butter a 2-inch high, 8-inch round cakepan.

Remove the layers from the refrigerator and let them rest on the counter for acouple of minutes before peeling away the plastic or paper. Fit one layer into thepan — if it breaks, just press the pieces together. If there's a little extra dough running up the sides of the pan, you can either fold it over the bottom layer orcut it so that it's even. Spoon some of the jam or pastry cream onto the dough,starting in the center of the cake and leaving one inch of dough bare around the border. Add more filling if you don't think it will squish out the sides when youpress down on it with the top layer of dough. (I find that 3/4 cup is usually justthe right amount, but if you're using a very thick jam, you might want a bit more.) Moisten the bare ring of dough with a little water and then top with thesecond piece of dough, pressing down around the edges to seal it. If you'd like,you can work your finger between the top dough and the edge of the pan, so that you tuck the dough under a little. Because of the softness of the dough and thebaking powder, even if you only press the layers together very lightly, they'llfuse as they bake. And, no matter how well you press them together, it seems inevitable that a little of the filling will escape.

Brush the top of the dough with the egg glaze and use the tips of the tines of afork to etch a cross-hatch pattern across the top.Bake the cake for 40 to 45 minutes, or until the top is golden brown. Transfer thecake to a cooling rack and let it rest for 5 minutes before carefully running ablunt knife around the edges of the cake. Turn the cake over onto a cooling rackand then quickly and carefully invert it onto another rack so that it can cool toroom temperature right side up.

Yogurt Cake

Ingredients

250 ml (1 cup) whole milk plain unsweetened yogurt (if you use two
125ml or 4oz tubs, you can use them to measure out the rest of the
Ingredients)
250 grams (2 cups) all-purpose flour (or 4 yogurt tubs)
2 large eggs
160 grams (3/4 cup plus 1 scant tablespoon) sugar (you can use an
empty tub of yogurt and measure the equivalent of 1 1/2 yogurt tubs if
you used the 125ml or 4oz kind)
80 ml (1/3 cup) vegetable oil (or a bit less than 1 yogurt tub)
1 1/2 teaspoon baking powder
1/2 teaspoon baking soda
1 teaspoon pure vanilla extract
1 tablespoon dark rum
a good pinch of salt

Instructions

1. Preheat the oven to 180° C (350° F) and line around 25-cm (10-inch)cake pan with parchment paper.
2. In a large mixing-bowl, gently combine the yogurt, eggs, sugar,vanilla, oil, and rum.
3. In another bowl, sift together the flour, baking powder, baking soda,and salt.

4. Fold the flour mixture into the yogurt mixture, mixing just until alltraces of flour disappear -- don't overwork the dough.

5. Pour the batter into the prepared cake pan, and bake for 30 to 35minutes, until the top is golden brown and a cake tester comes outclean.

6. Let stand for 10 minutes, then transfer to a rack to cool.

French Apple Tart

Ingredients

12 tbsp. unsalted butter, cubed and chilled 1¼ cups flour, plus more for dusting 7
Golden Delicious apples, peeled, cored, and halved ¼ tsp. kosher salt ½ cup
apricot jam ¼ cup sugar
Whipped cream or vanilla ice cream, for serving

Instructions

1. Combine flour, 8 tbsp. butter, and salt in a food processor and pulse until pea-size crumbles form, about 10 pulses. Drizzle in 3 tbsp. ice-cold water and pulseuntil dough is moistened, about 3—4 pulses. Transfer dough to a work surfaceand form into a flat disk; wrap in plastic wrap and refrigerate for 1 hour. Unwrapdough and transfer to a lightly floured work surface. Using a rolling pin, flatten dough into a 13″ circle and then transfer to a 11″ tart pan with a removablebottom; trim edges; chill for 1 hour.

2. Heat oven to 375°. Working with one apple half at a time, thinly slice intosections, keeping slices together. Press sliced apple half gently to fan it out;repeat with remaining apple halves. Place 1 fanned apple half on outer edge of the tart dough, pointing inward; repeat with 7 more apple halves. Separateremaining apple slices. Starting where the apple halves touch and working yourway in, layer apples to create a tight rose pattern. Fill in any gaps with remaining

apple. Sprinkle with sugar and then dot with remaining butter. Bake until goldenbrown, 60—70 minutes.
3. Meanwhile, heat apricot jam in a small saucepan until warmed and loose; pourthrough a fine strainer into a small bowl and set aside. Transfer tart to a wirerack; using a pastry brush, brush top of tart with jam. Let cool completely beforeslicing and serving with whipped cream.

Tarte au citron

Ingredients

*grated zest of one lemon, preferably unsprayed 1/2 cup (125 ml) freshly-
squeezed lemon juice 6 tablespoons (85 g) butter, salted or unsalted, cut into bits
1/2 cup (100 g) sugar 2 large egg yolks 2 large eggs
One pre-baked 9-inch (23 cm)*

Instructions

Preheat the oven to 350F (180C.) 1. In a medium-sized non-reactive saucepan,heat the lemon juice, zest, sugar, and butter. Have a mesh strainer nearby.

2. In a small bowl, beat together the eggs and the yolks.

3. When the butter is melted, whisk some of the warm lemon mixture into theeggs, stirring constantly, to warm them. Scrape the warmed eggs back into thesaucepan and cook over low heat, stirring constantly, until the mixture thickens and almost begins to bubble around the edges.

4. Pour the lemon curd though a strainer directly into the pre-baked tart shell,scraping with a rubber spatula to press it through.

5. Smooth the top of the tart and pop it in the oven for five minutes, just to setthe curd.

6. Remove from the oven and let cool before slicing and serving.

French strawberry pie

Ingredients
1 quart strawberries
1 package (3 ounces) cream cheese
1 baked pastry shell, 9-inch
1 1/4 cups granulated sugar
3 tablespoons cornstarch
1 tablespoon lemon juice
1/2 cup heavy cream
1 tablespoon confectioners' sugar
red food coloring

Preparation
Wash, drain, and hull strawberries. Beat cream cheese with a fork until smooth.Spread cream cheese over bottom of the cooled pie shell. Stand half of the wholestrawberries in the shell with tips up. Mash remaining strawberries; press through a sieve to remove seeds. Measure the strawberry juice, and if necessary,add water to make 1 1/2 cups of liquid. In a saucepan, mix granulated sugar with cornstarch; gradually stir in the strawberry juice mixture and the lemon juice.Cook over medium heat, stirring constantly, until thickened and clear, about 5 to7 minutes. Stir in a few drops of red food coloring; remove from heat. Cool sauce for about 10 minutes, then pour over the strawberries in the shell. Chill forabout 3 hours, or until firm. Beat cream with confectioners' sugar until mixtureholds its shape. Spoon

whipped cream in a ring around the edge of the pie. Storeleftover pie in the refrigerator.

Basque Pumpkin Cornbread

Ingredients

1 cup milk
1 cup puréed pumpkin
¼ cup sugar
1 tablespoon butter
½ teaspoon salt
2 cups cornmeal
1 tablespoon light or dark rum,
optional
3 eggs, room temperature, separated

Instructions

Butter a cake pan (7 inches round and 4 inches height), line the bottom withwax paper and butter the wax paper. I didn't have a cake pan with thesedimensions so I used a stainless-steel saucepan of a similar size.

Preheat your oven to 375°F.

Pour the pumpkin purée in a large bowl. In a small saucepan, heat the milk,butter and sugar on low heat, stirring constantly until the butter has melted. Pour the milk mixture to the pumpkin. Add the cornmeal ½ cup at a time, stirring toblend thoroughly. Stir in the salt.

Add the egg yolks to the pumpkin mixture and blend thoroughly using aspatula. Stir in the rum if using. In a separate mixing bowl, beat the egg whiteswith a hand mixer until stiff. Fold the egg whites into the batter.

Pour the batter into the prepared pan. Bake on the middle shelf of your oven forabout an hour, or when a knife inserted in the center comes out clean. If yourknife comes out wet, bake for another 10 minutes.Allow to cool for 20 minutes before unmolding. Slice into thin servings and serve warm.

Canelés

Ingredients

30 g (2 tablespoons) semi-salted butter, diced
500 ml (2 cups) milk
100 g (3/4 cup) all-purpose flour
1 vanilla pod, split, or 1 teaspoon vanilla extract or
paste
180 g (1 cup minus 2 tablespoons) sugar
1 teaspoon fine sea salt
80 ml (1/3 cup) good-quality rum
3 eggs

Instructions

1. Combine the milk, butter and vanilla in a medium saucepan, andbring to a simmer.
2. In the meantime, combine the flour, salt, and sugar in a mediummixing-bowl.
3. Break the eggs in another, smaller bowl, and beat gently withoutincorporating air.
4. When the milk mixture starts to simmer, remove from heat, fish outthe vanilla pod if using, and set aside to cool for 15 minutes.
5. Pour the eggs all at once into the flour mixture (don't stir yet), add inthe milk mixture, and stir until well combined (do not whisk).
6. Scrape the seeds from the vanilla pod with the dull side of a knifeblade, and return the seeds and pod to the mixture. Add the rum andstir.

7. Let cool to room temperature on the counter, then cover andrefrigerate for at least 24 hours and up to 3 days.

8. The next day (or the day after that, or the day after that), preheat theoven to 250° C (480° F).

9. Butter the canelémolds if they are made of copper (unnecessary ifyou're using silicon molds). Remove the batter from the fridge: it willhave separated a bit, so stir until well blended again, withoutwhisking or incorporating air.

10. Pour into the prepared molds, filling them almost to the top.

11. Put into the oven to bake for 20 minutes, then (without opening theoven door) lower the heat to 200° C (400° F) and bake for another 30to 40 minutes, depending on your oven and how you like yourcanelés.

12. The canelés are ready when the bottoms are a very dark brown, butnot burnt. If you feel they are darkening too fast, cover the molds witha piece of parchment paper.

13. Unmold onto a cooling rack (wait for about 10 minutes first if you'reusing silicon molds or they will collapse a little) and let cool
completely before eating.

Bugnes

Ingredients
250 g (14 fl. oz.) all purpose flour
50 g (slightly less than 1/2 stick or 4 tbsp) unsalter butter
50 g (2 fl. oz.) sugar
2 eggs
1 tbsp orange blossom water (optional)
salt
about 1/2 liter (1/2 quart) sunflower oil to deep-fry the bugnes.
powdered sugar (a few tablespoons)

Instructions
Prepare the dough at least 2 hours in advance:
1. Sift the flour over a large bowl.
2. Combine with the sugar, orange blossom water and a pinch of salt. Add the butter in very small parcels and mix a little.
3. Dig a hole (in french we say "unefontaine" -a fountain) in the centerof the flour mix. Beat the eggs and pour in the hole.
4. With the hands, combine all the Ingredients and knead for only aminute or two, until the dough gets homogenous.
Make a ball out of itand let it rest for at least 2 hours at room temperature under a cleancotton cloth.
5. Roll out the dough (on a flat, floured surface) as thinly as possible(about 2 mm) in a somewhat rectangular shape. This

should be fairlyeasy as the dough should be elastic and moist.

6. Cut out stripes about 1 1/2" to 2" wide. Divide the stripes into smallerrectangles, approximately 4" long. The bugnes on the pictures aresmall but feel free to make the stripes longer or wider if you prefer.Bugnes come in various sizes.

7. Twist the rectangles as follows:

1. With a knife, make a 1 1/2" long slit in the center of each rectangle, lengthwise.

2. Take one of the rectangle's small sides through this hole and reshape, as shown on the pictures above.

3. If you go with longer stripes of dough, there might be enough length to make two knots.

8. Heat the oil in a frying pan (oil should be about 1" or 1 1/2" deep)until boiling hot. Place a few knotted stripes of dough in it, makingsure they don't touch eachother.

9. Flip once, after only a few seconds, then wait a few seconds longer(this goes fast!).

10. Take out as soon as the bugnes have a nice golden (but not too dark)color. Drain on paper towels placed in a plate.

11. Once all the bugnes are cooked, sprinkle with powdered sugar (it'seasier to sprinke evenly if you use a small strainer and shake it overnthe bugnes).

Navettes de Marseille

Ingredients
200 g of sugar
500 g flour
3 CS orange flower water
6 tablespoons olive oil (about 50 ml)
2 eggs
1 teaspoon natural orange extract or zest of one orange
Milk to glaze shuttles
1/2 teaspoon salt

Directions

Start by beating the eggs and sugar until frothy property Add salt, orange flowerwater, extract or orange zest and olive oil Gradually add the flour, then finishedworking the dough by hand to get a nice ball Leave the dough ball one hour. Cut out your ball of dough into pieces the same size (I made 16 shuttles for me). Shape your shuttles (roll each piece into a sausage 10 cm long, pinch the endsand split the shuttle with a knife in length) Bake in hot oven (180 ° C) for 20 minutes Leave to cool. Keeps well in an airtight container.

Profiteroles

1/2 stick butter
1/2 cup water
1/2 cup all-purpose flour Pinch salt
Pinch ground cinnamon 2 eggs
Chocolate Sauce, recipe follows Ice cream
Chocolate Sauce
Special Equipment: Pastry bag fitted with large straight tip
1/4 cup heavy cream
4 ounces semisweet or dark chocolate 1 tablespoon corn syrup 2 tablespoons
butter 1 good pinch ground cinnamon

Preheat oven to 425 degrees F.

In a small saucepan combine the water, butter and salt and bring to a boil.Reduce the heat and add the flour all at once and stir it vigorously with a woodenspoon. Cook until the mixture has formed a ball and has a slightly sweaty sheen to it and it has pulled away from the pan. Transfer the mixture to a mixing bowland let cool for 3 to 4 minutes. The mixture does not have to be cold, just cool enough not to cook the eggs when added. Using an electric mixer or lots of goodold-fashioned elbow grease, beat in the eggs 1 at a time. Do not add the secondegg until the first is fully incorporated. Add in the cinnamon and beat for another second to combine.

Transfer the mixture to a pastry bag equipped with a large straight tip and pipe 1-inch balls onto a sheet tray lined with parchment paper. When done dip your finger in water and smooth the top of each ball where the pastry bag released the dough. Be sure to leave at least 1-inch between each of the balls. They grow! Bake in the preheated oven for 20 to 25 minutes, rotating the tray halfway through the cooking time to insure even cooking. When done, the puffs should be light, airy and dry inside. Cool on a rack.

When ready to serve, cut in half horizontally and fill with ice cream of your choosing. (I prefer a really high-quality vanilla.) Top with warm chocolate sauce. Bring a saucepan with 1-inch of water to a boil. Put the chocolate in a metal or heatproof glass mixing bowl and place on top of the saucepan with boiling water. Pay careful attention that the mixing bowl does not touch the surface of the boiling water. Add the rest of the Ingredients and stir until the chocolate has melted and everything is combined. This is a pretty quick process, once the chocolate has melted remove it from the double boiler set up. Spoon over the filled profiteroles. This is best when served warm!

A Beaumes de Venise cake

Ingredients
1 1/2 cups all purpose flour
Olive oil
1 teaspoon salt
1 teaspoon baking powder
3/4 cup plus 2 tablespoons sugar
1/4 teaspoon baking soda
3 tablespoons extra-virgin olive oil
8 tablespoons (1 stick) unsalted butter, room temperature
1 teaspoon grated lemon peel
2 large eggs
1 teaspoon vanilla extract
1 teaspoon grated orange peel
1 1/2 cups red seedless grapes
1 cup Beaumes-de-Venise or other Muscat wine

Preparation
Preheat oven to 400°F. Brush 10-inch-diameter springform pan with olive oil.Line bottom of pan with parchment; brush parchment with olive oil.Sift flour and next 3 Ingredients into bowl. Whisk 3/4 cup sugar, 6 tablespoons butter and 3 tablespoons oil in large bowl until smooth. Whisk in eggs, bothpeels and vanilla. Add flour mixture alternately with wine in 3 additions each, whisking just until smooth after each addition. Transfer batter to prepared pan;

smooth top. Sprinkle grapes over batter.Bake cake until top is set, about 20 minutes. Dot top of cake with 2 tablespoons butter; sprinkle 2 tablespoons sugar over. Bake until golden and tester insertedinto center comes out clean, about 20 minutes longer. Cool in pan on rack 20minutes. Release pan sides. Serve slightly warm or at room temperature.

A tartetropézienne

Orange Blossom Filling: 7 tablespoons sugar
2 sheets gelatine
3 egg yolks
5 tablespoons flour
2 1/2 cups milk
1/4 teaspoon salt
1/2 vanilla bean, split and scraped One 3-inch piece orange
peel 3 teaspoons
orange blossom water, divided 3/4 cups (1 1/2 sticks)
unsalted butter 1/2 cup
cream
Brioche:
2 1/2 teaspoons fresh yeast 3 tablespoons milk, divided 3
tablespoons sugar
2 1/3 cups all-purpose flour 4 eggs, divided
3/4 teaspoon salt
1/2 cup plus 2 tablespoons (1 1/4 sticks) unsalted butter, cut
into 1-inch pieces,
at room temperature 1 egg yolk
2 cups quartered strawberries Pearl sugar
1/4 cup chopped pistachios

To make the orange blossom filling, soak the gelatine in a
large bowl of cold

159

water. Whisk together the sugar, flour, egg yolks, and salt in a heat-proof bowl.

Whisk in the milk, orange peel, and vanilla bean seeds and pod. Place the bowl over a double boiler over medium heat and whisk constantly until the mixture

has come to a boil and thickened, about 7 minutes. Whisk in the butter, piece by piece, until it is all incorporated. Remove from the heat. Remove the gelatine

from the water and squeeze gently to remove any excess water. Add the gelatine to the egg mixture and whisk until smooth. Strain through a fine-mesh sieve.

Whisk in 2 teaspoons of the orange blossom water. Chill overnight.

To make the brioche, combine 1 tablespoon of the milk with the fresh yeast and whisk until smooth. In the bowl of a stand mixer fitted with a dough hook

attachment, combine the flour, sugar, and salt on low speed. Add the remaining milk, 3 of the eggs, and the egg yolk; increase the mixer speed to medium and

mix until the dough becomes a bit webby, about 1 to 2 minutes. Add the yeast

mixture and continue mixing until a ring of dough is left on the sides of the bowl, about 5 minutes. Add the butter piece by piece, letting each piece fullyincorporate before adding the next. Once all of the butter is incorporated, turnthe mixer speed up to medium-high and mix for 20 to 30 minutes, until thedough forms a ball on the dough hook and keeps itself there.

160

Lightly oil a large bowl and place the dough in it. Cover with plastic wrap andlet sit at room temperature for 1 1/2 hours, until the dough doubles in size. Chillfor at least 3 hours and up to overnight.

Place the dough on a lightly floured surface. Using a rolling pin, roll the doughinto a 1-inch-thick circle. Trim off the edges to make an 8-inch disk. (You cansave the scraps to make mini brioche buns.) Transfer the dough to a parchment-lined sheet tray. Combine the remaining egg with 2 tablespoons of water. Brushthe top and sides of the dough with the egg wash. Let the dough sit at roomtemperature until it doubles in size, about 50 minutes. Preheat the oven to 325°Fwhile you wait for the dough to proof.Brush the dough once more with the egg wash and generously sprinkle all overwith pearl sugar. Bake for approximately 15 minutes, rotating the brioche every5 minutes. The finished brioche should have an internal temperature of 200°F.Remove from the oven and let come to room temperature.To assemble the tarte, combine the remaining orange blossom water with thecream. Whip the cream until it forms medium peaks, then fold in the chilledorange blossom mixture in 2 additions. Using a serrated knife, cut the brioche inhalf horizontally. Spread a generous layer of the filling onto the bottom half ofthe brioche; sprinkle with strawberries and pistachios. Top with the upper half ofthe brioche. Refrigerate for 30 minutes before slicing and serving.

Macaron

Ingredients

For the Macarons
1 cup confectioners' sugar 3/4 cup almond flour 2 large egg
whites, room
temperature Pinch of cream of tartar 1/4 cup superfine
sugar
Fillings for Macarons
Chocolate: Chocolate Ganache
Coconut: 1 cup Swiss Meringue Buttercream, mixed with 1/3
cup
angel-flake coconut.
Peanut: Chocolate Ganache, or store-bought dulce de leche,
jam, or
peanut butter.
Pistachio: 1 cup Swiss Meringue Buttercream, mixed with
1/3 cup
finely chopped pistachios.
Raspberry: 3/4 cup seedless raspberry jam

Directions

Pulse confectioners' sugar and almond flour in a food
processor until combined.Sift mixture 2 times.
Preheat oven to 375 degrees. Whisk whites with a mixer on
medium speed untilfoamy. Add cream of tartar, and whisk
until soft peaks form. Reduce speed tolow, then add
superfine sugar. Increase speed to high, and whisk until stiff

peaksform, about 8 minutes. Sift flour mixture over whites, and fold until mixture issmooth and shiny.

Transfer batter to a pastry bag fitted with a 1/2-inch plain round tip, and pipe3/4-inch rounds 1 inch apart on parchment-lined baking sheets, dragging pastrytip to the side of rounds rather than forming peaks. Tap bottom of each sheet onwork surface to release trapped air. Let stand at room temperature for 15minutes. Reduce oven temperature to 325 degrees. Bake 1 sheet at a time, rotating halfway through, until macarons are crisp and firm, about 10 minutes.

After each batch, increase oven temperature to 375 degrees, heat for 5 minutes,then reduce to 325 degrees.

Let macarons cool on sheets for 2 to 3 minutes, then transfer to a wire rack. (Ifmacarons stick, spray water underneath parchment on hot sheet. The steam will help release macarons.)Sandwich 2 same-size macarons with 1 teaspoon filling. Serve immediately, orstack between layers of parchment, wrap in plastic, and freeze for up to 3months.

French Almond Nougat

Ingredients

For the mazetta
3/4 cup light corn syrup
2 large egg whites, room temperature
1/2 cup sugar
For the nougat
1 1/2 cups light corn syrup
1 teaspoon pure vanilla extract
1 1/2 cups sugar
4 tablespoons unsalted butter, melted
3 1/2 cups whole raw almonds, skin on
1/4 teaspoon salt

Directions

1. Begin by making the mazetta: Using an electric mixer, beat eggwhites until stiff; set aside. In a 1-quart saucepan, combine cornsyrup, 1/4 cup water, and sugar. Clip on a candy thermometer. Bringto a boil over high heat, stirring with a wooden spoon, about 5minutes. Wash down sides of pan with a pastry brush dipped in waterto remove any sugar crystals.

2. Cook over medium heat, stirring occasionally, until temperaturereaches 242 degrees (soft-ball stage), 15 to 20 minutes. Remove sugarsyrup from heat. Beating constantly on medium speed, slowly pourhot syrup into egg whites.

Continue beating for 3 to 4 minutes untilsyrup is incorporated. Use immediately or cover and refrigerate until ready to make the nougat.

3. Spray an 8-inch square baking pan with vegetable-oil spray; set aside.Place mazetta in a large bowl; set aside. In a 2-quart saucepan,combine corn syrup and sugar. Clip on candy thermometer. Bring to aboil over high heat, stirring constantly with a wooden spoon, 5 to 10minutes. Wash down sides of pan with a pastry brush dipped in water to remove any sugar crystals.

4. Over medium-high heat, cook to 280 degrees (soft-crack stage), 12 to15 minutes, without stirring. If heat is too high it can boil over, sowatch carefully. Remove from heat; let stand for 2 minutes. Withoutscraping pan, pour syrup over mazetta. Working quickly, stir with awooden spoon until almost smooth. Stir in butter, vanilla, and salt.

Mix until butter is incorporated. Stir in nuts. Scrape into preparedpan, and smooth the top; you may spray your hand with vegetable-oilspray and run it over the warm candy to smooth it. Let stand at roomtemperature, uncovered, until firm, 4 to 6 hours.

5. Spray a large cutting board generously with vegetable-oil spray.Unmold nougat from pan onto sprayed surface. Cut nougat into 3-by-1-by-3/4-inch pieces or other desired shapes. Wrap each piece incellophane or waxed paper.

Religieuse

Ingredients

60g/2¼oz butter, cut into cubes
75g/2½oz plain flour
2 free-range eggs, lightly beaten
For the crème pâtissière filling
75g/2½oz caster sugar
20g/¾oz cornflour
25g/1oz plain flour
500ml/18fl oz full-fat milk
1 vanilla pod, seeds only
6 medium free-range egg yolks
For the chocolate ganache icing
150ml/5fl oz double cream
200g/7oz plain chocolate (around 36% cocoa solids) broken
into
pieces
For the collar
150ml/5fl oz double cream

Method

1) Preheat the oven to 220C/425F/Gas 7. Line a baking tray with bakingparchment and draw onto it eight circles 5cm/2in wide and another eightcircles 2.5cm/1in wide. Put the butter in a heavy-based saucepan with150ml/5fl oz of water and heat over a medium heat until the butter melts.
Bring the mixture to the boil and then immediately remove from the heat.

2) Quickly tip in the flour. Stir vigorously with a wooden spoon until themixture forms a soft ball. Return to the heat and cook over a low heat for 3-5minutes, stirring constantly.

3) Remove from the heat and leave to cool slightly. Gradually add theeggs, beating well between each addition to form a smooth, shiny paste.Spoon the mixture into a piping bag fitted with a 1.5cm/ ½in plain nozzle.

4) Pipe round discs onto the baking tray in the marked circles and, using adamp finger, smooth over the top of each disc. Bake in the centre of the ovenfor 10 minutes. Reduce the oven temperature to 190C/375F/Gas 5 and cookfor a further 10-15 minutes. Remove the choux buns from the oven and pierceeach bun with a skewer to allow the steam to escape. Return to the oven for4-5 minutes to dry out. Remove from the oven and leave to cool on a wirerack.

5) For the crème pâtissière filling, pour the milk and vanilla seeds into aheavy-based pan and bring gradually to the boil. Remove from the heat andleave to cool for 30 seconds. Meanwhile, in a medium bowl, whisk togetherthe egg yolks and caster sugar until pale, then whisk in the cornflour andplain flour. Pour the vanilla-infused milk onto the eggs, whiskingcontinuously, then pour back into thepan.

6) Bring back to the boil, whisking continuously over a medium heat andcook for one minute. Pour the crème pâtissière into a bowl. Cover the surfacewith cling film to prevent a skin from forming and leave to cool. Transfer to the fridge to chill.

7) For the chocolate ganache icing, bring the cream to the boil in a smallpan. Remove from the heat. Add the chocolate

and stir until melted andshiny. Transfer to a bowl and leave to cool. Transfer the fridge to chill until the ganache has thickened to a spreadable consistency.

8) To assemble the religieuse, spoon the cold crème pâtissière into a pipingbag fitted with a long thin nozzle (or alternatively you can use a jam syringe).Fill the choux buns with the crème pâtissière.

9) Dip the filled buns into the chocolate ganache to coathalf-way up thesides. Sit the small buns on top of the larger buns.

10) For the collars, whip the cream in a mixing bowl until soft peaks formwhen the whisk is removed from the bowl. Spoon the cream into a piping bagfitted with a small star nozzle. Pipe lines of cream around the join where thesmall bun sits on top of the large bun to form a collar.

Fig tart

Ingredients

Frangipane 75g whole almonds (about 1/2 cup)
75g sugar, you can use half granulated sugar and half
confectioner's sugar, or
just all granulated sugar (about 1/8 cup granulated plus 1/4
cup confectioner's,
or just 1/3 cup granulated)
75g butter at room temperature
1 large egg

Method

Preheat the oven to 350F (180C). Spread the almonds evenly on a baking sheet and place them in the oven. Roast them for about 10minutes, or until slightly toasted anfragrant. Transfer to a plate and let cool toroom temperature.

Put the cooled almonds and the sugar into a food processor and process untilfine. Add the butter and the egg and pulse until well-combined. If you don'twant to use it right away, divide the frangipane into four equal parts, wrap each tightly in plastic. They will keep in the fridge for a couple of days, and up to amonth in the freezer.

To make a 9″ fig tart1 9″ pastry doughabout 10 large figs or about 15 small ones1/4 the recipe of frangipane above Preheat the oven to 400F (200C). Roll out your pastry dough to about 10-inch diameter – more or less won't harmanything. Spread about 1/4 of the quantity of

frangipane on the dough, leavingabout 1 inch parameter
around the outer edge of the dough. Quarter the figs
(only halve if small) and arrange them -pointy end up will be
prettier-inconcentric circles to cover the frangipane. Fold the
edges in, pinching a little tomake sure they stick. If you
want, you can brush the dough with eggwash and
give it a good shower of sugar. Bake for about 45-50
minutes, or until the pastryedges are golden brown. When I
feel like it I use a microplane to zest a meyerlemon right
over the tart just after it's out of the oven for an extra kick.

Gateau Saint-Honore

Ingredients

For the Pate Feuilletee (Puff Pastry)
2 cups (4 sticks) unsalted butter, chilled and cut into very small pieces
1 pound all-purpose flour, plus more for rolling out dough
1 large egg, lightly beaten
1 teaspoon salt
For the Pate a Choux (Cream Puffs)
1 1/2 cups all-purpose flour
7 tablespoons unsalted butter
7 large eggs
Pinch of salt
For the CremePatissiere (Pastry Cream)
1 vanilla bean, split
6 large egg yolks
1 cup milk
1 cup heavy cream
1/2 cup granulated sugar
3 tablespoons all-purpose flour
For the Caramel
1 1/4 cups granulated sugar
3 tablespoons corn syrup
For the Creme Chantilly (Whipped Cream)
4 cups heavy cream
3/4 cup confectioners' sugar
1 teaspoon vanilla extract

Directions

1. Weigh the flour accurately. In the bowl of an electric mixer fittedwith the paddle attachment, beat the butter until smooth. Add 1/2 cupflour; mix until smooth. Scrape this butter mixture onto a piece ofwaxed paper. Form into a 5-inch square, wrap; transfer to therefrigerator until chilled.

2. Place remaining flour in mixer bowl; add 1 cup water and salt. Mixcarefully into a smooth dough, being careful not to overmix. Gatherdough into a ball, and wrap in plastic. Chill a few minutes.

3. On a lightly floured surface, roll out the dough into a 6-by-12-inchrectangle. Place the chilled butter square in the center of the rectangle.Fold over the dough, completely encasing the butter. Press the edgesof the dough together, sealing as well as possible. Transfer to a sheetof waxed paper; chill until dough and butter reach same temperature.

4. On a lightly floured surface, roll out dough into a 3/8-inch-thickrectangle. Fold into thirds, like a letter, and roll into another 3/8-inch-thick rectangle. Transfer dough to waxed paper, and chill 1 hour. (Tryto use as little flour as possible for the rolling, and brush off anyexcess before folding dough.)

5. Repeat rolling-and-folding process two more times; chill 1 hour. Rolland fold two more times. When you fold the dough for the sixth time,the dough should be extremely smooth and silky, with no lumps ofbutter visible. (If the dough becomes too elastic, set aside in a coolplace 15 to 20 minutes before rolling.)

6. Divide dough in half. Wrap each half in plastic wrap. Refrigerate onehalf for the Gateau Saint-Honore, and freeze the other half for lateruse.

7. Line a baking sheet with parchment paper; set aside. Heat the oven to375 degrees.

8. Combine the butter and 1 cup water in a small saucepan, and set overhigh heat. Bring to a boil, and immediately add the flour and salt.Beat continuously with a wooden spoon until the dough comes awayfrom the sides of the pan.

9. Transfer the mixture to the bowl of an electric mixer. Using thepaddle attachment, add the eggs, one at a time. Reserve 1 1/2 cupsdough for assembling the cake.

10. Place remaining mixture in a pastry bag fitted with an Ateco #9824tip. Pipe 1-inch balls, spaced 1 1/2 inches apart, on the preparedbaking sheet.

11. Bake balls until dark-golden brown, 40 to 45 minutes. Transfer to awire rack to cool. Set 18 balls aside; freeze remaining balls in anairtight container for another use.

12. Using a small paring knife, make a small hole in the bottom of eachball. Set aside.

13. Combine the milk, heavy cream, and vanilla bean in a mediumsaucepan. Set pan over medium heat, and scald the milk mixture.Remove the pan from heat, cover, and let mixture steep 10 to 12minutes. Remove and discard the vanilla bean.14. In a small bowl, whisk together the egg yolks and the sugar until lightand fluffy, about 2 minutes. Add the flour, and continue whisking eggmixture until smooth.

15. Slowly pour the hot milk mixture into the egg mixture. Whisk thisnew mixture until it is completely smooth and completely free oflumps.

16. Return new mixture to pan, and place over medium heat. Bringmixture to a boil, whisking constantly; cook 2 minutes more.

17. Transfer the pastry cream to a bowl. Lay a piece of plastic wrapdirectly on top of the pastry cream to prevent a skin from forming.Refrigerate until ready to use.

18. Place half of the pastry cream in a pastry bag fitted with an Ateco #6round tip; reserve the remaining pastry cream for assembling thecake. Pipe pastry cream into each of the 18 reserved balls. Set thefilled cream puffs aside until you are ready to dip them in the caramel.

19. Prepare an ice-water bath, and line a baking pan with parchment; setboth aside.

20. Combine the sugar, 1/4 cup water, and corn syrup in a smallsaucepan. Set over high heat, and bring to a boil. Swirl the panoccasionally until the sugar has dissolved. Continue cooking until thesyrup is golden-amber. Remove pan from heat, and plunge bottom ofpan in the ice bath to stop cooking.

21. Dip the top of each of the 18 filled cream puffs in the molten caramel.

Place the balls, top-sides down, on the prepared baking sheet; thecaramel will harden and flatten, and this surface will become the topof the cake.

22. Place a sheet of parchment paper on a clean work surface. Using asmall offset spatula, place a small amount of molten caramel on theparchment. Starting from the center, draw out the caramel in a fewquick strokes, creating a fan. Repeat making more fans with theremaining caramel.

23. Set fans aside to harden and dry. Remove from the parchment, anduse for garnish.

24. In the bowl of an electric mixer fitted with the paddle attachment,combine the heavy cream, confectioners' sugar, and vanilla. Beat onhigh speed until the mixture forms stiff peaks, 2 to 3 minutes. Chilluntil ready to use.

25. Heat the oven to 375 degrees. Line two baking sheets with parchmentpaper, and set aside.

26. Roll the dough out to an 1/8-inch thickness. Using a plate or a bowl asa guide, cut out two 8-inch circles from the dough. Prick the circlesall over with a fork or a pastry docker to prevent the dough fromrising. Place the circles on the prepared baking sheets. Brush the outeredge of the circles with the beaten egg.

27. Place the reserved pate a choux dough in a pastry bag fitted with anAteco #9824 tip. Pipe dough around the rim of each circle. Withremaining dough, pipe a spiral in the center of each circle, starting inthe middle.

28. Bake until the pastry is crisp and deep-golden brown, 50 to 55minutes. Transfer baking sheets to a rack to cool.

29. Dip uncoated sides of cream puffs, one by one, in the caramel. Arrange 9 per circle, leaving space in between; the caramel will holdthe cream puffs to the pastry.

30. Combine the remaining pastry cream and one-fourth of the crème chantilly in a bowl. Place the mixed cream in a pastry bag fitted withan Ateco #9824 tip. Fill the center of each circle with cream mixture.

31. Place the remaining crème chantilly in a pastry bag fitted with anAteco #9824 tip. Pipe large rosettes between the caramel-coveredcream puffs. Cover the center of each circle with the remainingcream. Garnish with caramel fans, and serve.

Madeleines

Ingredients

1/2 teaspoon double-acting baking powder
3/4 cup (95 grams) all-purpose flour
1/2 cup (100 grams) sugar
2 large eggs, at room temperature
2 teaspoons vanilla extract
Grated zest of 1 lemon
5 tablespoons (2 1/2 ounces; 70 grams) unsalted butter,
melted and cooled

Directions

Sift together the flour and baking powder and keep close at hand. Working in amixer fit with the whisk attachment, beat the eggs and sugar together onmedium-high speed until they thicken and lighten in color, 2 to 4 minutes. Beat in the lemon zest and vanilla. Switch to a large rubber spatula and gently fold inthe dry Ingredients, followed by the melted butter. Cover the batter with plastic wrap, pressing the wrap against the surface to create an airtight seal, and chill forat least 3 hours, perhaps longer–chilling helps the batter develop itscharacteristic crown, known as the hump or the bump. (The batter can be kept tightly covered in the refrigerator for up to 2 days.) Center a rack in the oven andpreheat the oven to 400 degrees F (200 degrees C). If your Madeleine pan is notnonstick, generously butter it, dust the insides with flour and tap out the excess.

If the pan is nonstick, you still might want to give it an insurance coating ofbutter and flour. If it is silicone, do nothing. No matter what kind of pan youhave, place it on a baking sheet for easy transportability.

Divide the batter among the molds, filling them almost to the top. Don't worryabout smoothing the batter, it will even out as it bakes.Bake large madeleines for 11 to 13 minutes, small ones for 8 to 10 minutes, oruntil the cookies are puffed and golden and spring back when touched. Pull the pan from the oven and remove the cookies by either rapping the pan against thecounter (the madeleines should drop out) or gently running a butte knife aroundthe edges of the cookies. Allow the madeleines to cool on a cooling rack. Theycan be served ever so slightly warm or at room temperature.

Savoy cake

Ingredients

1 1/2 cups (200g) powdered sugar
6 large eggs, separated
1 1/2 teaspoons vanilla extract
1/4 cup (60ml) boiling water
1/4 teaspoon cream of tartar
1/2 teaspoon salt
optional: 1/2 cup (50g) finely chopped candied angelica
1 cup (150g) cake flour

Directions

Softened butter and additional powdered sugar for preparing the pan

1. Toss the angelica with a bit of the flour to separate the pieces and set aside.
2. Butter a 10-inch (27cm) bundt pan and dust the inside with powdered sugar,then tap out any excess.
3. Preheat the oven to 300°F (150°C.)
4. In the bowl of a stand mixer, stir together the egg yolks with the sugar. Whipthe yolks on high speed until thick and lightened in color. With the mixerrunning on high speed, dribble in the very hot water, a few teaspoons at a time, then add the vanilla. Continue whipping until the mixture has rethickened andresembles soft pudding, holding its shape when you lift the whip.

5. In a separate bowl, whip the egg whites with the salt and cream of tartar untilthey hold stiff peaks.

6. Put the cake flour in a mesh strainer or sifter, and sprinkle the flour over theyolks, folding it into the yolks gradually as you sift.

(If you're not so dexterous, scrape the whipped yolks into a larger bowl, set thebowl in the center a damp kitchen towel formed into a circle on the countertop,and use one hand to sift in the flour and the other to fold it in.)

7. Stir in the candied angelica then fold in one-third of the beaten egg whitesuntil fully incorporated. Then fold in the remaining egg whites.

8. Scrape the batter into the prepared pan and bake for 1 hour. It's done when atoothpick inserted into the center comes out clean, with perhaps just a fewcrumbs attached. Remove from oven and immediately turn the cake out onto a wire cooling rack.Let cool completely before slicing.

Fromage Blanc

Ingredients

2 quarts whole milk, as fresh as possible
1 cup heavy cream (optional)
2 cups fresh buttermilk
2 tablespoons fresh lemon juice, strained
1/4 to 1/2 teaspoon salt, if desired
Heavy Cream, for serving

Directions

In a large, heavy saucepan, add the milk and the cream for a richer fromageblanc. In a mixing bowl, combine the buttermilk and lemon juice and stir tocombine well. Add the buttermilk-lemon juice mixture to the milk and begin to heat the milk, over low heat and very slowly, to 175 degreesF°. While the milk isheating, stir only twice, making 2 strokes each time, with a heat-proof spatula orother flat utensil. Check the temperature often. As soon as the temperaturereaches 175 degrees F, remove the pot from the heat and allow to sit,undisturbed, for 10 minutes.
Line a large colander with 2 layers of fine cheesecloth and set over a large bowl.Gently ladle the curds and whey into the colander and allow to drain until thedrips of whey slows, about 2 minutes. Tie the corners of the cheesecloth togetherto form a hanging pouch, and hang pouch over a bowl and allow to drain untilthe cheese reaches the desired consistency.

Serve as is, with preserves, honey or fresh fruit, or add salt or fresh herbs, totaste, and enjoy as a savory appetizer. If a rich cheese is desired, spoon or pour abit of heavy cream over the top before serving. Also, if a very smooth product is desired, beat the cheese briefly with an electric mixer before serving.Refrigerate until ready to serve, up to 1 week. If cheese is marinated in oil withfresh herbs, it will keep, refrigerated, for up to 1 month.

Chocolate Mousse

Ingredients
3/4 cup chilled heavy cream, divided
4 large egg yolks
1/4 cup espresso or strong coffee, room temperature
3 tablespoons sugar, divided
6 ounces semisweet chocolate (60-72% cacao), chopped
2 large egg whites
1/8 teaspoon kosher salt

Preparation
Beat 1/2 cup cream in medium bowl until stiff peaks form; cover andchill.

Combine egg yolks, espresso, salt, and 2 Tbsp. sugar in a large metalbowl. Set over a saucepan of gently simmering water (do not allowbowl to touch water). Cook, whisking constantly, until mixture islighter in color and almost doubled in volume and an instant-readthermometer inserted into the mixture registers 160 degrees, about 1minute. Remove bowl from pan. Add chocolate; whisk until melted andsmooth. Let stand, whisking occasionally, until room temperature.Using an electric mixer, beat egg white in another medium bowl onmedium speed until foamy. With mixer running, gradually beat inremaining 1 Tbsp. sugar. Increase speed to high and beat until firmpeaks form. Fold egg whites into chocolate in 2 additions; fold whipped creaminto mixture just to blend.

Divide mousse among six teacups or 4-oz. ramekins. Chill until firm,at least 2 hours. DO AHEAD: Mousse can be made 1 day ahead;cover and keep chilled. Let stand at room temperature for 10 minutesbefore serving.
Before serving, whisk remaining 1/4 cup cream in a small bowl untilsoft peaks form; dollop over mousse.

Kouglof Alsatian Brioche

Ingredients

50 grams (1/4 cup) sugar
300 grams (10 1/2 ounces, see note) flour
120 ml (1/2 cup) lukewarm milk
15 grams (1/2 ounce) fresh yeast (for other types of yeast, see substitutions)
1 tablespoon dark rum or kirsch
3 eggs, lightly beaten
a good pinch salt (I used demi-sel butter so I skipped this)
120 grams (1/2 cup plus 1 tablespoon) butter, at room temperature and diced, plus a good pat for the mold
45 grams (1/3 cup) raisins and/or sultanas, soaked overnight in warm water or tea and drained
35 grams (1/2 cup) sliced almonds
confectioner's sugar for dusting
a few whole almonds or a little more sliced almonds for the mold

Instructions

1. Combine the flour and sugar in a large mixing bowl. In a small bowl,combine the fresh yeast with the milk and stir to soften. Form a wellin the flour and pour in the milk mixture, eggs, and rum. Mixeverything in with a wooden spoon.

2. Mix the dough vigorously for 10 minutes, add the softened dicedbutter, and continue working with the dough another 10 minutes orso, until it becomes elastic. Be warned

that brioche dough is verysticky; if you have a stand mixer with a dough hook, now would be agood time to use it. Add the sliced almonds and drained raisins, and
mix again to combine.

3. Cover the bowl with a kitchen towel and let the dough rise for 30minutes in a warm spot of the house (I opted to place it on a kitchentowel on top of the radiator). After the first rise, punch the doughdown and knead it briefly again.

4. Butter the pan generously and right up to the top. Place a wholealmond in each groove of the mold (or sprinkle with more slicedalmonds). Pour the dough into the mold and return it to the warmspot.

5. Let the dough rise to fill the mold, about 1 hour.

6. Preheat the oven to 180° C (360° F) with a heat-resistant cup of waterplaced on the oven rack. Put the kouglof in the oven and bake for 45minutes, until crusty and brown, and until a knife inserted in thecenter of the dough comes out clean. If the top seems to brown toofast, protect it with a piece of foil or parchment paper.

7. Let cool completely on a rack, about 2 hours, before unmolding.

8. Dust with confectioner's sugar and serve with jam, honey, or maplebutter. Kouglof keeps for a few days, tightly wrapped in a cleankitchen towel; slices can be toasted to refresh their texture. You canalso freeze part or all of the loaf.

Mont Blanc

Ingredients

For the meringue

150g/5¼fl oz free-range egg whites (approximately 5 egg whites)

300g/11oz caster sugar

2 tspcornflour

1 tsp white wine vinegar

For the caramelised nuts

vegetable oil, for deep frying

100g/3½oz caster sugar

100ml/3½fl oz water

110g/4oz mixed unsalted nuts

sea salt flakes

For the filling

110g/4oz dark chocolate

500g/1lb 2oz sweetened chestnut purée

1 vanilla pod, seeds only

175g/6oz caster sugar

300g/11oz mascarpone

250ml/9fl oz double cream

8-12 marronsglacés (candied chestnuts), crumbled

For the caramel

150g/5¼oz caster sugar

1 tbsp water

Preparation

1. For the meringue, preheat the oven to 140C/275F/Gas 1. Line abaking tray with greaseproof paper.

2. Whisk the egg whites in a clean bowl until soft peaks form when thewhisk is removed.

3. Whisk in the sugar, a spoonful at a time, until all of the sugar hasbeen added and stiff peaks form when the whisk is removed.

4. Whisk in the cornflour and vinegar.

5. Spoon the meringue mixture onto the baking tray in a large circle.

6. Bake in the oven for 10 minutes, then switch the oven off and leave inthe oven for 2-3 hours, or preferably overnight, until crisp, butuncoloured.

7. Remove the meringue from the oven and set aside to cool completely,then place onto a serving plate.

8. Meanwhile for the caramelised nuts, heat the oil in a deep heavy-based frying pan until a breadcrumb sizzles and turns brown whendropped into it. (CAUTION: hot oil can be dangerous. Do not leaveunattended.)

9. Heat the sugar and water in a separate saucepan until the sugar hasdissolved.

10. Add the nuts and bring the mixture to the boil. Continue to cook untilthe temperature of the sugar syrup reaches 110C/225F (use a sugarthermometer to check this).

11. Remove the nuts from the syrup using a slotted spoon and carefullylower them into the deep fat fryer. (CAUTION: The nuts are coated ina liquid that may spit upon contact with the oil. Stand well back and

keep your face and hair away from the deep fat fryer.) Fry for 1-2minutes, or until golden-brown, then remove from the oil using aslotted spoon and set aside to drain on kitchen paper. Sprinkle withsea salt flakes.

12. For the filling, melt the chocolate in a bowl set over a saucepan ofboiling water. (Do not let the base of the bowl touch the water.)

13. Smooth the melted chocolate over the cooled meringue.

14. Whisk the sweetened chestnut purée, vanilla seeds, caster sugar andmascarpone in a bowl until combined.

15. Whisk the cream in a separate bowl until soft peaks form when thewhisk is removed. Fold the double cream into the chestnut mixture.

16. Spoon the chestnut mixture onto the meringue and scatter the marronsglacés and caramelised nuts on top.

17. For the caramel, heat a frying pan until hot, add the caster sugar andwater and cook for 4-5 minutes, or until the mixture becomes a palecaramel. (Do not stir the mixture.)

18. Drizzle the caramel over the top to serve.

Männele (St. Nicholas Bread)

Ingredient
For the mannele
500g flour
5g salt
90g sugar
200ml milk
30g fresh yeast
2 eggs
100g butter
For glaze and finishing
1 egg
2.5ml powdered sugar
2.5 ml milk
raisins
For the icing (optional)
100g icing sugar

Method
1. Combine the flour, salt and sugar in a bowl.
2. Warm 100 ml (6 tbsp.) milk in a saucepan; pour it into a bowl.
3. Dissolve the yeast in the warm milk; add 100 g (3 1/2 oz.) flour andmix well. Cover with a clean cloth and let rise 20 minutes.
4. In a saucepan, melt the butter with the remaining milk, sugar and saltwithout boiling. Remove from the heat and cool to lukewarm.

5. Knead the butter-milk mixture into the yeast starter.

6. Incorporate the whole eggs and the rest of the flour. Knead well for10-15 minutes. Cover the bowl with a clean cloth and let rise 30minutes.

7. Transfer the dough to a floured board; form into small cylinders 3 cmin diameter and 15 cm long.

8. Using scissors, make cuts to form the head, arms and legs so that thedough will have a gingerbread-man shape.

9. Place the männele on buttered baking sheets; glaze with the beatenegg yolk (or egg yolk beaten with a little milk and sugar).

10. Form the eyes and nose with raisins. Let rise 20 minutes more.

11. Bake in a preheated 180°C / 350°F oven for about 25 minutes or untilnicely browned.

Damson pie

Ingredients
225g fresh damsons, washed
55g caster sugar
360ml double cream
75ml milk
1 tbsp honey
6 egg yolks
1 x 20cm shortcrust pastry case, baked blind

Method
1. Stew the fruit with the sugar and 50ml cold water until soft
but not breaking apart. Drain in a sieve.
2. Warm the cream, milk and honey in a saucepan over a medium heat. Just before boiling, pour onto the egg yolks and whisk together until smooth.
3. Scatter the stewed fruit into the pastry case, place on a baking tray and slowly pour over the custard mixture. Bake in the oven (180^C) for about 30 minutes until set.

Tarte Frangipane Mirabelles

Ingredients

For the crust:

5 tablespoons (70gr) unsalted butter, at room temperature 3 egg yolks

pinch salt

1/2 cup (80gr) superfine sweet white rice flour 1/2 cup (60gr) millet flour 1/4

cup (30gr) sorghum flour 1/4 cup (40gr) corn starch 1/2 teaspoon xanthan gum 2

tablespoons to 1/4 cup cold water (optional if the dough seems too dry) For the

filling:

1 stick (115 gr) butter, softened 1/3 cup (115gr) honey

1 cup (100 gr) ground almonds (blanched, slivered, whole, your call) 2 eggs

1/4 cup (60gr) heavy cream 1/4 teaspoon cardamom

1-2 cups pitted mirabelles plums (or your preferred stone fruit)

Method

Prepare the crust: In a mixer, whip the butter on medium speed until light andairy. Add the egg yolks, one at a time and beating well after each addition. Mixuntil incorporated. Add the salt, and all the different flours, and the xanthamgum and mix briefly. Add some water, one tablespoon at a time if the doughfeels too dry. Dump the whole mixture onto a lightly floured (use more rice flour) board and gather the dough into a smooth ball. Flatten the dough into adisk, wrap it in plastic wrap and refrigerate for an hour.Preheat oven to 350F and position a rack in the center.When the dough is nice and cold, roll it out on a lightly floured board or inbetween two sheets of plastic to fit your prefered pie pan. If the dough tearswhile you roll or/and transfer into the pan, just patch it with your fingertips. Linethe dough with a piece of parchment paper, fill with pie weights or dy beans andpar bake for 10-15 minutes until almost completely baked. Remove the weightsand parchment paper. At this point you can refrigerate the baked crust for up to 3days before using.

Prepare the almond filling and mirabelles topping: Place the butter, honey,ground almonds, and the eggs in a large bowl and whisk until smooth (can alsobe done in a food processor). Add the cream and cardamom but stir in it insteadof whisking not to emulsify it or it will rise while baking.Arrange the mirabelles halves at the bottom of the pie crust and pour the creamover them. Bake 25-30 minutes at 350F. Drizzle with a bit of extra honey ifdesired when still warm.